A Fireside Moment with God

A Collection of Poems that Will
Inspire and Challenge Your Heart

Shirlisa Christner Harris

CROSSBOOKS

CrossBooks™
A Division of LifeWay
1663 Liberty Drive
Bloomington, IN 47403
www.crossbooks.com
Phone: 1-866-879-0502

All illustrations were created and provided by:
Ben Penton
BP Interactive
1017 Summerfield Drive
Maryville, TN 37801
Phone: 865-201-0677

©2011 Shirlisa Christner Harris. All rights reserved.

Cover photography provided by Devon Murphy, dmurphy031@gmail.com

Cover modeling provided by Lauren Carpenter.

No part of this book may be reproduced, stored in a retrieval system, or transmitted by any means without the written permission of the author.

First published by CrossBooks 04/19/2011

ISBN: 978-1-6150-7628-4 (sc)
ISBN: 978-1-6150-7627-7 (dj)

Library of Congress Control Number: 2010940541

Printed in the United States of America

This book is printed on acid-free paper.

Because of the dynamic nature of the Internet, any Web addresses or links contained in this book may have changed since publication and may no longer be valid. The views expressed in this work are solely those of the author and do not necessarily reflect the views of the publisher, and the publisher hereby disclaims any responsibility for them.

Dedicated to …

*… my husband, Steve,
and our four precious children,
Shireena, Stevie, Scottie, and Shelby*

*… and to all those
who desire an occasional nudge
along the road of life
in moving toward truth,
toward courage,
toward hope…
toward GOD.*

Table of Contents

DEDICATION v

THANK YOU x

INTRODUCTION. xii

Let Jesus Walk with You 1

The Ultimate Friendship 3

The Other Side of Waiting 7

What Is Life? 11

For Now — or Forever? 17

Loneliness — God's Opportunity 25

God Knows Best 31

The Divine Design 35

Help for the Hurting Heart 43

Have Faith in a Faithful God 49

Tried and Purified 51

Looking Unto Jesus 61

Making a World of Difference 65

By Chance or by Choice? 69

Dying to Live 77

Our Heavenly Father's Care 83

A Heartbeat of His Handiwork 87

A Journey of the Heart. 95

Saved by Hope. 99

The Essence of God's Presence 109

Destined to Die? 113

Trampled Treasures. 121

America: From Triumph to Tragedy 129

Come, Lord Jesus. 135

Where Are You, Lord? 137

Sweeter as the Waves Go By 143

When Only God Knows 151

Suffering — the Path to Perfection 155

Serving the Lord is an Honor. 159

I Prayed for You 163

Natural Remedies for Unnatural Maladies 167

The Heart of the Matter. 171

The Freedom of Forgiveness 177

A Trust to Treasure 183

A Farewell to Friends 187

So You're Sweet Sixteen 189

None Other Like Mother. 193

The Gift of a Dad	199
I Miss You	207
A Mission of Love	211
Introduction	212
Our Story	214
A Tiny Glimpse of Heaven	228

THANK YOU ...

... to all those sweet family members and friends,
who have coached and encouraged me these many years,
and whose welcome input has helped in creating numerous parts of this book
which may otherwise not have been.
I love you!

... to the pastors and church members of
Gospel of Life Outreach of Sturgis, Michigan,
Christian Outreach of Sturgis, Michigan,
Christ Temple of Kalamazoo, Michigan,
and First Apostolic Church of Maryville, Tennessee,
for urging and inspiring me forward when a creation
such as this still seemed so far out of reach.
I appreciate you!

... to Pastor Kenny and Penny Carpenter,
of First Apostolic Church of Maryville,
for working so hard to create the kind of amazing environment
in which a book such as this could be born.
You are awesome!

... to Ben Penton,
my patient graphic designer with BP Interactive,
for doing such a remarkable job in providing the beautiful
illustrations contained in this book. You are a complete Godsend!

… to Devon Murphy and Lauren Carpenter,
for adjusting your busy schedules enough to provide
the desired effects for the front cover of this book.
Your generous display of both talent and skill
made the difference.

… to Jon Lowell Lineback, Beth Ludema,
Jason Klarke, Stefanie Holzbacher, David Orr,
and the rest of the team at CrossBooks,
who have been invaluable in helping to make
all of this happen. You've been great and I couldn't
have done so well without you!

… to my brother-in-law and sister,
Mike and Sheryl Virgil,
for the hands-on assistance which you willingly provided
over the years. You've contributed more to the fabric
of this book than what you can know.
Mit viel Liebe und Dank!

… most of all, to my beloved Savior, Jesus Christ,
without Whom I would not be where I am today,
and without Whose faithful love I would not have known
the hope, peace, and fullness of life which I gratefully enjoy today.
To God be the glory!

INTRODUCTION

It was spring in our rural farming community of southwest Michigan. The year was 1979, and I was a sophomore in high school. I had been given an English assignment of writing a poem of choice—not a picture, a short story, or an essay, but a poem. Initially, I hesitantly wondered what I could write that would contain the quality or significance required to receive a good grade. However, within a few minutes of pondering quietly, I picked up my pencil and began to write the words of a poem, which I would later entitle "Let Jesus Walk with You." For some reason, I saved it, and that became the beginning of a journey I had never envisioned for myself; one through which God would begin to reveal His heart to me, thereby profoundly impacting my heart, my soul, and my life.

As the years began to pass and my life took on additional interests, there were seasons in which I wrote nothing of note. Then there were other times when I would finish one poem and move right on to another. As I grew in God and began to experience more of life, I eventually recognized when the hand of God was touching my heart in a special kind of way—thereby inspiring the words by which someone might be encouraged in taking another step, in believing that there was hope beyond the present hardship, and in embracing the awareness that Jesus really cared. Some poems began as a thought quickly scribbled onto a piece of scrap paper and stuck away, only to be rediscovered a few experiences later with new insight ready to add to its contents. Others began with good momentum, only to be stopped short by writer's block. Many months, and sometimes a disappointment or two down the road, I would pick up my pen and begin to write again, because it was time … and I was ready. The moment for completion had come.

As with all of life, there is a seasoning process by which we are prepared for service, and all with the purpose of making a difference for the kingdom and glory of God. Without Jesus, we are nothing; neither can we do anything of enduring substance or quality. The sooner we submit ourselves to that reality, the sooner God can use our lives with the kind of effectiveness in changing the world around us as *He* desires for it to happen.

As you read the contents of this book, you will be reading pieces of the last thirty years of my life, pieces that reflect the infilling of God's sweet presence, His patience, His mercy, and His faithful love. It is my desire that you enjoy what you read, that you be challenged in considering another way of thinking from the Bible's point of view, and most of all, that your heart will be drawn closer to Jesus in the unfathomable love shown toward you since the beginning of time and creation. Because after everything else is said and done, that is all that really matters.

"For of [God], and through [God], and to [God], are all things: to Whom be glory for ever. Amen" (Romans 11:36 KJV).

Shirlisa Christner Harris

Let Jesus Walk with You

*One is never so alone as when he attempts
to walk life's road without God.*

When the road ahead seems dark
and encouragements are few,
Just fix your eyes on Jesus
for He wants to walk with you.

Through every storm and tempest,
let Jesus lead the way;
He'll take your hand to guide you,
and walk with you each day.

He's always good and faithful
and to everyone so true;
When He reaches out in kindness,
won't you let Him walk with you?

*I will walk among you and be your God,
and you shall be My people.*
Leviticus 26:12 NKJV

The Ultimate Friendship

True friendship is the threads of two lives
which have been entwined by the hand of God
and fashioned into a cord of strength.

Deep in the heart of every man
is a longing for someone to care
About a great mountaintop reached in his life
or a burden that he's had to bear.

With a friend by his side, the load seems much lighter,
the mountains to climb aren't so steep;
The nights are less fearsome, and rivers to cross
don't appear quite so wide and so deep.

A hand on the shoulder, a small word of cheer,
can quickly drive dark clouds away;
A prayer sent to heaven can be the umbrella
that shields on a cold, rainy day.

With a friend of true worth comes the comfort and joy
of sharing your innermost feelings;
Your times of communion will be like a balm
bringing hope and a sweet inner healing.

The words that you speak do not need to be measured
nor hurts falsely hidden in pride;
This friend of pure excellence shares in your joys
and understands times when you cry.

Though spoken expressions will clearly reveal
the smallest of imaginations,
Mere understood silence between you can mean
you've a bond that's without obligations.

There may also be times when a friend in his love
will in kindness reach out to reprove,
Because of a wrong road you chose as the right
or a deed you desired to do.

With bravery accept it, be grateful in heart,
for 'twas said by the wisest of men,
That *an enemy's kiss overflows with deceit,*
but faithful are the wounds of a friend.

When prosperity wanes and your wealth seems like sand
that slips through your tightly-closed hand,
Many a man who spoke highly of you
may turn and then from you disband.

But the one who is made of the finest of gold,
though from you he received ne'er a dime,
Through sunshine and rain he will always stand by you—
a true friend will love at all times.

Yet down through the ages and over the pathway
of life which so many have trod,
There's never been found a more true, lasting friendship
as when a man walks with his *God.*

*A man that hath friends must show himself friendly:
and there is a Friend that sticketh closer than a brother.*
Proverbs 18:24 KJV

The Other Side of Waiting

*Patience is the inner quality
by which I accept a difficult situation from God
without giving Him a deadline to remove it.*
    Bill Gothard

When walls surround you, doors are barred,
you seem to wait alone,
Look up to God—you'll soon behold
new ways you've never known!

Hold fast your faith in valleys low,
with hope your mountains climb;
This path you'll oft not understand,
but it's by God's design.

With hands so kind, He'll touch your eyes
and draw the veil aside,
Transforming thus your earthly view
to those things glorified.

And as your faith turns into sight,
God's plan begins unfolding;
Those times of waiting, He will say,
were times of greatest molding.

*The fiery trials of your faith
you know as tribulations;
But I used them to nurture you
in meekness, trust, and patience.*

*The work which I've ordained for you
requires strength and power;
In waiting, you were seasoned
in your calling for this hour.*

*You're now prepared to walk through doors
that once seemed to be closed;
As you've surrendered to My plan,
you've opened like a rose.*

*If I had kept back but one part
to lighten just one test,
I would have done so at your cost
and given you less than best.*

*So bloom where I've placed you, and rest in the fact
that I always complete what I start;
Just wait upon Me, and be of good courage,
and surely I'll strengthen your heart.*

*Wait on the Lord; be of good courage,
and He shall strengthen your heart;
wait, I say, on the Lord.*
Psalm 27:14 NKJV

What Is Life?

*Life is a daily preparation
for that which lies beyond today.*

What is life? A question asked
that's echoed through the ages;
What is one's worth when for his toil
death is earth's final wages?

Can life be measured with a gauge
whose needle moves but once?
Or by a calendar whose days
melt swiftly into months?

The sun, a clock, an hourglass
with steady silence pace
Each fleeting second of precious time
of this, life's final race.

The young and old, the great and small,
down life's short path come teeming,
Each with a single quest in mind—
to find life's real meaning.

The search goes on, no one's exempt,
not kings or theologians,
Housewives, farmers, carpenters,
or sailors on the oceans.

A baby's cry, a child's laugh,
a youthful stride to stardom …
Then with such rapid ease comes age
like frost on summer's garden.

The rich man dies and leaves his wealth
to he who hasn't earned it;
The scholar leaves his find with those
who labored not to learn it.

Then what's the worth of hoarded wealth,
of monuments and fame?
Just as the grass, a man returns
to dust from whence he came.

Such brevity of time, this life—
a whisper in the night;
A shadow faint, then quickly gone,
as darkness swallows light.

It's as the dust before the wind,
a breath, a feeble sigh;
A vapor rising in the breeze
that fades into the sky.

It's as a flower of the field
that blooms for just a time,
And as a fruit that softly falls
from off an autumn vine.

As then the value of a life
as just a passing story?
Or did the wise Creator wish
to use it for His glory?

Each day's a gift from God's own hand,
the blessings are but borrowed;
Each moment is a training ground
preparing for tomorrow.

Our thoughts and motives, words and deeds,
are much like threads we weave
Into a garment made in time
to wear eternally.

And in the purpling hue of life,
as time and timeless meet,
What will one's best be worth when laid
at his Creator's feet?

Just as the mountains meet the sky
and waters meet the shore,
So will a man meet with his God,
when time shall be no more.

Will God then see you from afar,
and say as Judge, *Depart!*
You had no time for Me on earth—
you never knew My heart?

*Or will He look through eyes of love,
and as your Savior say,
I know you well, oh, faithful one—
My child, come home to stay?*

*For a thousand years in Thy sight are but as yesterday
when it is past, and as a watch in the night.
So teach us to number our days,
that we may apply our hearts unto wisdom.*
Psalm 90:4, 12 KJV

For Now — or Forever?

*Will my influence die with me, or will it
joyfully resonate within the immortal souls
of those who come behind me?*

Beneath a blazing sunrise,
bathed in shades of pink and red,
A sleepy world begins to stir—
a new day waits ahead.

The curtains of a midnight gray
are briskly thrust aside;
And from the brilliance of the light,
the darkness flees to hide.

But then how quickly comes the dusk
and draws night's shades once more;
And on another day of life,
it softly shuts the door.

Just as a page within a book
turned by a gentle wind,
So stealthily, the day is gone—
it can't be lived again.

Each spoken word and feeling,
thoughts which occupied the mind,
Are substance which can never be
retrieved from space and time.

Were singing birds, bright azure skies,
or freshly furrowed sod,
A flower, or a rippling brook,
a quiet talk with God,

A part of that one day, now gone?
'Twas given by the hand
Of He Who made the Universe
with but His word's command.

Or was the day a frenzied maze
of people, cars, and phones,
Appointments, pressures, mind-encumbering
past-due bills and loans?

Were cutting and unfeeling words,
a thoughtless deed in haste,
Results of stress which turned some precious
moments into waste?

Convenient foods, appliances,
the instant, throw-away,
Have never made life easier
than what it is today.

But yet we have less time to spend
on things of lasting worth,
Like helping others, seeking God,
for family, and for church.

Moms and dads, immersed in work,
leave children far behind,
Who'll bear the scars for life
because for them was little time.

The years pass swiftly ... these same parents
find themselves alone,
And wonder why their children
seldom call or visit home.

There's nothing can replace the strength
and worth of family ties,
Created by much time and love,
which money never buys.

Providing for one's household
and the poor is good, indeed;
But many seek *more* than enough,
exemplifying greed.

I've got to go! I'm busy!
I don't have the time to spare!
Are phrases common in our days
of quiet moments rare.

In search of life's fulfillment
scampers all humanity,
For pleasure, power, wealth,
which without God are vanity.

A host of social functions,
which our feverish pace comprise,
Will never stand the test of worth
when weighed with lost souls' cries.

Where are the people called by God,
who once would intercede
Before the throne of mercy,
for a weary soul in need?

We just can't find the time to pray—
the schedule is so full!
But we'll take time for late night shows
or Sunday's Super Bowl.

Society is steeped in themes
of *go* and *do* and *be;*
But ultimately, God will ask,
How well do you know Me?

Though with your hands you labor much,
your feet go many places,
Relationship's the key wherein
your heart with Mine embraces.

Communion brings a likeness
of the spirit, heart, and soul,
A oneness of desire,
and a singleness of goal.

It doesn't happen easily—
commitment is required:
A dying to your will
and many things which you've desired.

And as your heart is emptied out
of everything but Me,
You'll know Me as your source of life,
your all-sufficiency.

To know Me is to love Me,
and to love is to obey;
I'll know how much you love Me,
if you keep the words I say.

In serving Me, your goal should not
for fame and greatness be;
But rather, that you lose your self
and find your life in Me.

Though much you'll do for My name's sake,
take heed to your own soul;
Lest in your zeal to occupy,
your love for Me grows cold.

The hours spent before Me
in a quiet place alone,
Are where you come to know Me
as I only can be known.

*Take time for Me in every day—
My will and plan pursue;
Remember back to Calvary …
when I took time for you.*

*For what will it profit a man
if he gains the whole world, and loses his own soul?
Or what will a man give in exchange for his soul?*
Mark 8:36, 37 NKJV

Loneliness — God's Opportunity

*Trying to find lasting fulfillment without God
is just as impossible as trying to imagine
a rainbow without color.*

Like icy winds across a plain
and cold rain on one's face,
Comes loneliness to many hearts
and occupies a place.

With feet upon the wings of time,
she comes when there's a hurt,
An insecurity or loss,
low feeling of self-worth.

To old and young, to rich and poor,
to famous and obscure,
She stretches forth her wrinkled hand—
her grip is firm and sure.

Let me abide inside of you,
I know just how you feel;
Then with an aged and raspy voice,
says she, *I'll make a deal.*

*Give me your hand and we will walk
through life unto its end;
You'll learn to cope like other folks
who've let me be their friend.*

*I'll not betray your feelings
or expose the times you cry,
Nor will I tell when you're distressed,
and ask the question, why?*

*A multitude of single folks
have hearkened to her when
They were convinced within themselves
that no one wanted them.*

*The fear of being left alone
then baits the hook and lure,
That leads young boys and girls to choose
what's peer instead of pure.*

*It's loneliness which oft creeps in
and leaves a marriage broken;
When thoughts suggest, You've known neglect—
forget the vows you've spoken!*

*Discouragement and hopelessness,
depression, fear, and grief,
Join hand in hand with loneliness
to ward off all relief.*

*But through the clouds there comes a voice,
alive with hope and peace:
Cast all your cares on Me,
and I will cause your storm to cease.*

Oh, weary, heavy-laden one,
down-trodden and oppressed,
Reach up and grasp My nail-scarred hand—
I'll lead you into rest.

For every trial you have known,
I've faced the same as well;
I've known the weight you've carried,
for beneath the cross I fell.

I've felt your hurts, I've known your pain,
I, too, alone have cried;
I've faced rejection from the world—
the world for whom I died.

I understand your loneliness
when I look 'round and see,
How people try to fill that void
with everything but Me.

Is there a care too great for Me,
a tear that I can't dry?
But, nay, I conquered death
with victory's banner flying high!

I, Jesus, am life's answer—
I'm the One Who loves your soul;
I with My life will change your life
and make the broken whole.

*I'll fill each void with just Myself,
and in you I will be
Your soul's contentment, hope, and joy,
and life abundantly.*

*For we do not have a High Priest who cannot sympathize
with our weaknesses, but was in all points tempted as we are,
yet without sin. Let us therefore come boldly to the throne of grace,
that we may obtain mercy and find grace to help in time of need.*
Hebrews 4:15, 16 NKJV

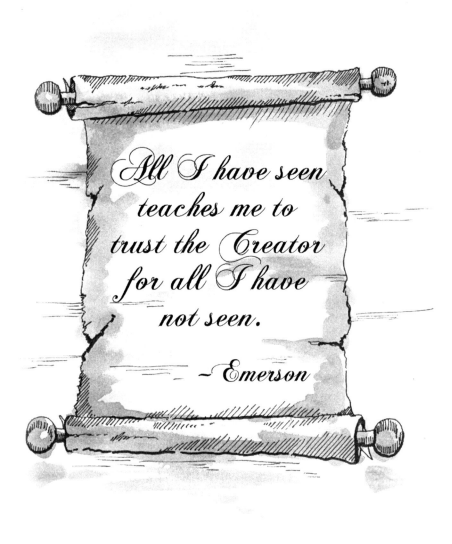

God Knows Best

Enough that God my Father knows:
Nothing this faith can dim.
He gives the very best to those
Who leave the choice with Him.
Unknown

Sometimes it's hard to understand
why things go like they do,
And why life can't continue
in a misty rainbow's hue.

And yet, the stately beauty
of a dew-kissed crimson rose
Is not alone of sunshine's rays
to warm it as it grows.

There must be also gray skies,
dismal clouds, and then the rain;
But through it all emerges life,
with luster unrestrained.

And so it is when changes fall
as shadows across our way;
It's difficult to see the good,
unless we've learned to pray.

And when God softly whispers *no*
to one of our requests,
He's no less loving, kind, and good
than when He's answered *yes*.

As anxiously the future
with the present we compare,
Why fear tomorrow when we know
that God's already there?

Just up ahead awaits
another part of His vast plan;
Trust wholly in His care for you,
hold tightly to His hand.

He sees far down the road,
'round every bend, o'er every hill;
And lovingly, He guides our lives
according to His will.

In time we'll understand it all,
but 'til then we must rest ...
Entrusting all to God
for now, as always, He knows best.

*And we know that all things work together for good
to those who love God, to those who are the called
according to His purpose.*
Romans 8:28 NKJV

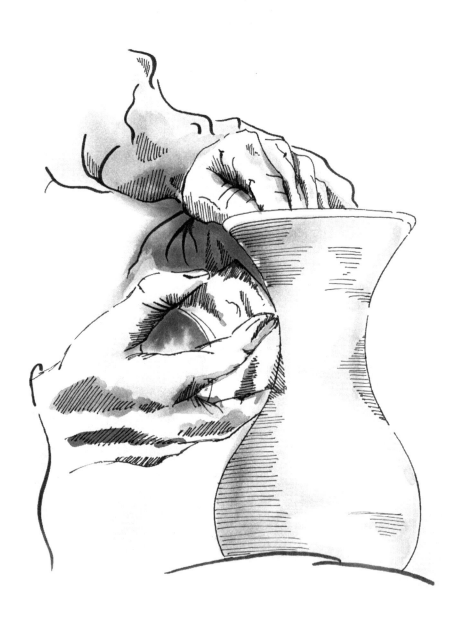

The Divine Design

There is an invisible Sculptor
Who chisels the face into conformity
with the attitude of the soul.
Unknown

From heaven's splendor, through the skies,
   a hand stretched toward the earth,
  And gently grasped a piece of clay
   which seemed of little worth.

The hand so large ascended slowly,
    dripping yet with mire;
  The eyes of He Who held the clay
    burned softly with desire.

Whose was this hand that reached far down,
   the mighty distance spanned,
  And from earth's darkness sought a life?
   It was the Potter's hand.

With hands adept, the Potter
  all debris and stone removed;
   Then added bits of flint,
so that its strength would be improved.

But then He seemed as though to throw
   the clay upon a wheel;
  And as the wheel began to turn,
   He softly said, *Just yield.*

There's much you will not understand
within My plan for you;
But e'er that plan can be fulfilled,
there's work that I must do.

Remain but soft and pliable
within My hand of care;
Don't harden 'neath the pressure,
for resistance brings a snare.

Though often progress will seem slow,
stay patient and surrendered;
For when you fight against My hand,
My work is greatly hindered.

With every turn the wheel makes,
I'll surely be at work;
The changes will seem frequent,
and at times you'll seem to hurt.

Amidst your sufferings, don't despair—
I have your best in mind;
And as I shape you, you'll become
a work of rare design.

As day by day the wheel turned,
the hand, with loving skill,
Began creating from the clay
a vessel He could fill.

At times the clay thought wearily,
This process seems too slow!
Or when the fingers pressed a bit,
Why do You make me so?

The water which You use on me
is just a bit too cold!
Is there no way to do without
and still my vessel mold?

My base formation most will say
is not acceptable;
It's much too flat and rigid—
I'll be thought inflexible!

Distinctly different is my shape—
I'm strange to look upon;
The marks You've etched into my sides
seem so misplaced and wrong!

The Potter sighed, then patiently
endeavored to explain:
Oh, earthen vessel, do not fret—
in trust there lies great gain.

The water is to keep you
from becoming rough and dry;
I could not shape you, you'd but break,
were I without to try.

Your base is your foundation—
it is flat so you can stand,
When strong winds blow and others
fall away on every hand.

The marks engraved upon you
are creative works of art,
Adorning you with character
and comeliness of heart.

Your vessel has a pouring spout
proportionate in size,
So I might fill and pour through you
to needy hearts and lives.

The vessel became still,
while listening to the Potter speak;
Then humbly said, *Just as You will,
let it be done with me.*

The Potter worked a little more,
then smiling, satisfied,
He set it on a shelf
where it would stay until it dried.

Then by and by He took a brush,
and with a gentle stroke,
Began concealing ugly gray—
and once again He spoke:

*I'm covering you with righteousness,
of choicest colors fair;
Where once was earthy gray,
'twill now be heavenly beauty there.*

*The Potter paused, then softly said,
But e'er you can be used,
This glaze which I've applied to you
must with your substance fuse.*

*With care, He lifted steadily
the trembling work of clay;
And toward the heated kiln,
He gently, slowly made His way.*

*The clay then pled, Oh, Potter,
must I through the fire go?
I'll be consumed amidst the heat—
I am but dust, You know!*

*The Potter opened up the door
and eased the clay inside;
And as the door closed, said, Endure,
that I be glorified.*

*Much time went by until one day,
He smiled, and said, 'Tis done!
And opening the door, exclaimed,
Come forth, my faithful one!*

With tenderness, He spoke,
as He again the vessel lifted:
*Now come and see the end of those
who stubbornly resisted.*

The Potter strode in silence
to a corner dark and cold,
Wherein there lay a broken mass
of vessels new and old.

*These are the ones who chose to go
the way of self-destruction;
I sought and chose them for My use,
but they refused instruction.*

*Some left My hand while on the wheel,
and some while being fired;
While others on the Master's table
said they got too tired.*

*Of all the broken vessels here,
but few will turn about
To let Me mend their broken lives …
the rest will be cast out.*

*They're of no value in this state—
they're vessels of dishonor;*
Then pointing with His finger,
He said, *Now, let us go yonder.*

𝒜nticipation filled the air
as they approached a place,
Where 'round a table spread so fair
sat those of every race.

𝒜midst this bounty did the Potter
set His vessel down,
And said, *You are now ready
to be filled and passed around.*

*𝒲ith patience, you endured
the fiery death to your affections,
Which has produced a shine
wherein I see My own reflection.*

*𝒲ith oil, I will fill you now,
and thereby flow through you;
And thus, with My anointing,
a transforming work I'll do.*

*𝒜ccording to My perfect plan,
I've wrought your life to be
A vessel unto honor,
giving glory back to Me.*

*But now, O Lord, Thou art our Father;
we are the clay, and Thou our Potter;
and we all are the work of Thy hand.*
Isaiah 64:8 KJV

Help for the Hurting Heart

*The most effective testimony is born
from the experience of a heart
and the transformation of a life.*

Is yours a heart that's heavy
with the weight of deep despair?
And as each day gives way to night,
you ask, *Does no one care?*

Depression, hatred, guilt, and pain,
from somewhere in your past,
Put hope's bright light far from your reach,
your soul with shadows cast.

Distress and anger, fearfulness,
rejections not a few,
Have now convinced your weary mind
life's best is not for you.

Another party, one more joint,
and one more shot of booze,
Bring short relief as you cry out,
Was I just born to lose?

Your money's gone, your friends are scarce,
your life is nearly wasted;
There is but little that you've not tried—
you've pain and pleasure tasted.

You've walked the shores of loneliness
and known cold waves of fear;
You've felt defeat's dark, crushing blow
when victory seemed so near.

Relationships with those once close
lie shattered at your feet;
The echo of your empty heart
mocks life with every beat.

But, wait! There *is* Someone Who cares;
your hurt and sadness feels,
Who understands each tear you cry,
and every heartache heals.

His sinless hands and feet, His back,
bear scars of sin and shame;
He loved the world that crucified Him—
Jesus is His name!

With outstretched hands, He gently pleads,
Won't you but give to Me
Your empty heart, your troubled life,
the hurts no one can see?

Your emptiness I'll wholly fill,
with peace dispel your fears;
Your hatred I will turn to love
and give you joy for tears.

And as I root out bitterness,
forgiveness will replace
The ugly wounds and anger,
which mere time could not erase.

The scars left by rejection
and the ache of loneliness
Will melt away as I engulf you
in my holiness.

I'll break depression's grip,
and from despair grant sweet release;
And then I'll flood you with enduring
comfort, hope, and peace.

You've sought in vain for meaning
in earth's pleasures quickly passing;
But I'll fulfill your searching heart
with life that's everlasting.

Your groping for life's answers
will be over, and you'll know
That I, alone, can wholly save
and satisfy your soul.

I'll pardon you of guilt and wrong,
if you'll but ask Me to;
Your burdens I will gladly bear—
I care so much for you!

*Though others leave, a faithful friend
I will forever be;
Through life I'll stay beside you,
if you'll choose to walk with Me.*

*The blood I shed was for your sins—
I paid your penalty;
For you I cried, in love I died …
now won't you live for Me?*

*In this the love of God was manifested toward us,
that God has sent His only begotten Son into the world,
that we might live through Him.*
I John 4:9 NKJV

Have Faith in a Faithful God

*The secret of faith that is ready for emergencies
is the quiet, practical dependence upon God day by day,
which makes Him real to the believing heart.*
Dr. Howard Taylor

The sparrow neither sows nor reaps
nor gathers into barns;
And yet, God feeds it daily,
sees each time it suffers harm.

The lily does not toil or spin,
yet quietly it grows;
And on its simple beauty,
rain and sunshine God bestows.

If He so cares for that which will
tomorrow pass away,
Oh, you of little faith,
will He not care for you each day?

*Do not worry about your life, what you will eat;
nor about the body, what you will put on.
If … God so clothes the grass, which today is in the field
and tomorrow is thrown into the oven,
how much more will He clothe you, O you of little faith?*
Luke 12:22, 28 NKJV

Tried and Purified

*The difficulties which we encounter
will leave their mark for a little time—
our responses to them will leave their mark forever.*

When trials vex my soul
and darkness hovers overhead,
When trouble is my water
and affliction is my bread;

When heartaches overwhelm me
and the road seems bleak and long,
When battles seem to increase
and my understanding's gone;

In perfect peace You'll keep me,
if my mind on You is stayed;
And though dark clouds are closing in,
I will not be afraid.

I'll bring to mind Your faithfulness,
Your answers when I cried;
Your steadfast love which held me,
when my soul by storms was tried.

Against these things I have no might
and don't know what to do;
But God, I will not be dismayed—
my eyes are fixed on You.

I shall instruct my heart
to be encouraged in You, Lord;
In thanking You for all these things,
my joy will be restored.

I see Your guiding hand within
each storm which comes to prove
The depth of my commitment
to be faithful and unmoved.

And having done all I can do,
I must yet firmly stand;
Your counsel will sustain me
and will be my heart's command.

More than a conqueror I am—
though not by might or sword—
But by the power, in the name,
of Jesus Christ, my Lord!

I'll still myself and see
the great salvation that You'll bring;
My help and hope are in Your name,
great God and mighty King!

And when I seek to understand,
You softly whisper, *Trust—*
My ways surpass your reasoning heart
and frail mind of dust.

Thus, when life's answers I don't have
or know which way to go,
Remind me, Lord, that I have You,
and You the answers know.

And when my mind is vexed with thoughts
which war against my soul,
When doubt and condemnation
have begun to take their toll;

Forsaking all vain reasoning,
I'll yield to Your control;
And cast my cares upon You,
faithful Keeper of my soul.

My feet You'll hold within Your steps—
You'll keep me in the way;
I will not slip or falter,
if I trust You and obey.

You order all my steps, oh Lord,
e'en when things seem so wrong;
And in life's hour of midnight,
I'll still sing the victor's song.

When scorned, rejected, this I know,
of You I'm not forsaken;
Cast down, I will not be destroyed
nor from Your love be shaken.

Sometimes I cannot feel You
from within or from without;
But in these times is when I learn
what faith is all about.

My feelings aren't dependable,
they seem to come and go;
Yet strengthened by things visible,
my faith they can o'erthrow.

It's faith which sees what can't be seen
and hears what can't be heard;
Prevailing over doubt and fear,
when founded on Your Word.

With truth You opened up my eyes,
where once there was but blindness;
You spared my life from death
and crowned my soul with loving kindness.

In mercy, You reproved me,
when I wandered carelessly;
Instruction I will not refuse,
for it is life to me.

Correction is not joyous,
but unto this word I cleave:
That whom You love You chasten,
and You scourge whom You receive.

When praying isn't easy
and my words seem cold and vain,
With diligence, I must pray on—
persistence dare not wane!

Before the victory comes the war,
the rainbow follows rain;
The night comes first and then the dawn,
and triumph after pain.

Relentless I must be
as I ascend life's rocky slope;
I must endure unto the end,
and never lose my hope.

For it's not he who starts that wins,
but he who perseveres
Through failure, disappointment,
hardship, fighting, pain, and fears.

And so I'll travel on through life
with You, Lord, as my Guide;
Through sorrow and adversity,
beneath Your wings I'll hide.

Amidst the dark uncertainties
of rivers I must ford,
I still can lift my hands and whisper,
Holy is the Lord.

Life's hardships are Your tools
to reveal to me my heart;
And tests are used as lamps
to search the hidden inward parts.

Please cleanse me, Lord, from secret faults
and keep me from all sin,
Lest I be drawn away from You
by fleshly lusts within.

If I resist the Tempter
by the Word of God, he'll flee;
And then when I draw near to You,
You will draw near to me.

Oh Lord, create in me a heart
for You that's clean and white;
Renew in me a spirit
that is holy, pure, and right.

My times are in Your hand, oh God,
on You my soul does wait;
You will perfect what You've begun—
Your work You won't forsake.

All things together work for good
to those who love You, Lord;
May Your desires be my joy,
Your presence my reward.

It's through much tribulation,
I, in faith and patience, grow;
And in my times of suffering,
strength and power You bestow.

Through suffering, I'm transfigured—
I'm perfected by Your fire;
Your silence tests my faithfulness
and fervor of desire.

From suffering I recoil,
and from pain myself I shield;
Yet these teach me obedience,
and cause my will to yield.

And when I wrestle with my will
and with desires strong,
May I become so lost in You …
until my will is gone.

And after I have suffered,
may the God of peace and grace
Perfect, establish, strengthen me,
and shine upon my face.

May there be but one heartbeat, Lord,
between Your heart and mine;
And wholly fill my life
with Your sweet Spirit, Christ Divine.

You know the pathway which I take,
through all my hand You'll hold;
When You by fire have tried me,
I'll come forth as purest gold.

And through eternal ages,
as my soul with praise does throb,
I'll thank You for Your wondrous works
and bless Your name, oh God!

But He knoweth the way that I take:
when He hath tried me, I shall come forth as gold.
Job 23:10 KJV

Looking Unto Jesus

*Don't look at Christ through your circumstances,
but look at your circumstances through Christ.*
Pastor Larry Pike

What is the answer for those times
when memories cloud one's face,
When wounds within the heart
seem like a chilling wind's embrace?
We then must gaze to skies beyond,
where sorrows find no place ...
And looking unto Jesus,
let Him every pain erase.

When disappointments come our way
and promises are broken,
When dreams lie shattered at our feet,
amends remain unspoken;
In searching through our tears,
we trace a shining rainbow's token ...
And looking unto Jesus,
peace engulfs us like an ocean.

At times, like small ships out at sea,
great doubts like billows roll;
Relentless seems the howling gale,
the night is long and cold;
With eyes upon the angry storm,
fear overwhelms the soul ...
But looking unto Jesus,
we can rest—He's in control.

Confronted by temptation,
oft like feeble prey we fall;
The shield of faith lies at our side,
our sword of truth's waxed dull;
Resisting fleshly passion,
we must for the right stand tall ...
By looking unto Jesus,
there is victory over all.

Our soul's dread foe encamps about,
around us fly his arrows;
He bids us seek a way more broad,
to shun this path so narrow;
But 'neath the wings of Him we'll hide
Who sees each falling sparrow ...
And looking unto Jesus,
distant seem the hovering perils.

And when this road we walk leads us
through valleys, betwixt stones,
Gone are the things familiar
and the loved ones we had known;
We'll cling to He Who died
with but a cross to call His own ...
And looking unto Jesus,
hear Him say, *You're not alone.*

Throughout our earthly pilgrimage,
the world pursues with cries:
*Content you'll be with beauty, fame,
and all that money buys!*
But mended hearts and rescued souls
see things through different eyes ...
For looking unto Jesus,
He completely satisfies.

And when our souls wing flight
beyond the skies where eagles soar,
When questions turn to vapor,
trifling cares are ever o'er;
We'll join angelic anthems
praising Him Whom we've adored ...
And looking unto Jesus,
we will hail Him King and Lord!

The stones which cut our feet will then
as gems our crowns adorn;
The tears we cried will crystals be,
our hearts as never torn;
We'll bow before those precious feet
that Calvary's cross had borne ...
Then ever look to Jesus
on that bright eternal morn.

*Looking unto Jesus, the author and finisher
of our faith; Who for the joy that was set before Him
endured the cross, despising the shame, and is set down
at the right hand of the throne of God.*
Hebrews 12:2 KJV

Making a World of Difference

*What duty views as an obligation,
love welcomes as an opportunity.*

How was the world made better
by my place in it today?
How did I make a difference
for some soul along the way?

Did I extend a hand to ease
the weight of someone's burden?
Or spend the night in prayer for one
whose progress seemed uncertain?

Did I, though weary, bravely smile
to a passerby?
Or offer words of comfort,
when within I felt to sigh?

And when a harsh word came my way
or wrong towards me was done,
Did I choose to forgive
and try to aid the faltering one?

When asked to render services
devoid of personal gain,
Did cheerfully I do them,
never thinking to complain?

And when I staggered 'neath a blow,
and thought, *How can I take it?*
Did I reach out to someone else,
with hope say, *You can make it?*

When one who long disdained me
reached a mountain's glistening crest,
Did I share in his jubilance,
though I'd experienced less?

And when I thought to criticize
another for his ways,
Did I instead find reasons
to divert to words of praise?

When cutting words escaped my lips
and caused a hidden injury,
Did I with deep contrition say,
I'm sorry—please forgive me?

Did I allow a stumbling block
to be my steppingstone?
And in the face of wrong,
did I choose right, though all alone?

Tough problems there will always be,
but none too hard to solve,
If in all things we will allow
the Lord to be involved.

The world will be a brighter place,
when selflessness shines through;
Dispelling clouds of darkness,
by the kindness that we do.

To first love God with all our heart,
soul, mind, and strength within,
And then all others as ourselves,
is where it all begins.

Real happiness and peace will follow,
as will true success;
For if we sow the seed God's way,
we'll reap His very best.

*As ye would that men should do to you,
do ye also to them likewise.*
Luke 6:31 KJV

By Chance or by Choice?

*One major mistake in an unguarded moment
could change your life forever,
and wreak emotional and spiritual damage
that a lifetime might not repair.*
Pat Boone

Does life begin by accident
and end by simply chance?
Are joys and sorrows on earth's road
by merely happenstance?

Are actions just a gamble,
random shots into the night?
Are stumblings due to ignorance
excuse for less than right?

We seem to be so slow to learn
from others' sad mistakes;
So oft we try to beat God's laws,
and thus, much life we waste.

Instruction and correction
to our pride are simply loathsome;
We sidestep words of wisdom,
and still trust for outcomes wholesome.

But problems stem quite often
from wrong choices we have made:
If we would have God's blessings,
then His laws must be obeyed.

God's principles were written
with our very best in mind;
But when we proudly go *our* way,
His best we never find.

In self-will and impatience,
many disregard advice;
Then wonder why their choices
carry such a heavy price.

We make our choices glibly—
Live and learn, we lightly say;
Yet pain and loss we might avoid,
if we'd learn first to pray.

God does not lay a snare for us
nor lead into temptation;
But lust and pride within our hearts
cause untold devastation.

What worth holds one small choice?
Will one bad move leave much to pay?
Life's pages of man's history
show us much about today.

In Eden's perfect beauty
were a man and woman placed,
Created in God's likeness
and first of the human race.

With them was left the right to choose
and exercise their will;
But what they chose brought sorrow,
thorns, and soil in sweat to till.

They hardly could have known
the vast results their choice would have
On countless generations,
who of flesh and bone were clad.

A life of beauty, priceless wealth,
in just a moment's time
Of one unguarded, unwise move,
were wrenched from all mankind.

'Twas not by chance that Adam sinned
with Eve in Eden's garden,
When Satan queried, *Hath God said?*
and doubt their conscience hardened.

But it was rather by their choice
and will to disobey,
That they exchanged true life for death
upon that tragic day.

A subtle speech, suggestion smooth,
and truth to error bent—
They learned so late, 'twas then as now,
that what God said, He meant.

And thus God gives to every soul
a choice of destiny;
Each has a lifetime to decide,
What of eternity?

Eternity—the human mind
can hardly comprehend;
It's timelessness ... forever ...
a beginning with no end.

Were one to count the grains of sand
upon each ocean's shore,
Or drain earth's rivers drop by drop
until there'd be no more;

Or if a bird would, leaf by leaf,
remove each tree's green robe,
'Twould be as but a breath in time
when ends this earthly road.

What horror comes to those who chose
to live a Godless life;
For all earth's pleasures, sensual thrills—
forever without Christ!

Gross darkness, torment, weeping, pain,
    and suffering undescribed,
Come not by chance, but by a life
    which God's sure Word defied.

And yet, how blessed the one who's walked
    with Jesus side by side,
In every area—none withheld—
    His wishes not denied.

What awesome glory, ageless bliss,
    to those who've known the Christ:
The One Who chose to give His life,
    to pay love's highest price.

Sweet heaven's best is their reward,
    God's radiance their glory;
That *Jesus Christ is Lord of all*
    will be their endless story.

Chance does not dictate what will be,
    but rather, each may choose;
And those who love and live for God
    won't be by Him refused.

What one must lose upon this earth
    to gain of heaven's best,
Can be compared to knowing life
    because one gave up death.

This life on earth, we live but once—
may this be our endeavor:
To know and walk with God,
because *eternity's forever.*

*I have set before you life and death, blessing and cursing;
therefore choose life, that both you and your descendants may live;
that you may love the Lord your God, that you may obey His voice,
and that you may cling to Him, for He is your life
and the length of your days.*
Deuteronomy 30:19b, 20 NKJV

Dying to Live

*Love for oneself results in the denial
of God and others—love for God and others
results in the denial of oneself.*

Alone again ... you've often wondered
what makes others leave,
And why so many overlook
your times of greatest need.

Why is it when you give your all
and do the best you can,
That in the end the credit's given
to another man?

You sacrificed and freely gave,
when others suffered loss;
Yet when you lost but life itself,
alone you bore your cross.

You loved though others hated you,
and blessed when you were mocked;
When words like stones were hurled at you,
you clung but to the Rock.

When others fought life's dragons,
you stayed with them to the end;
But when the night for you stretched long,
mere silence was your friend.

You bore the shame with patient grace,
    when you were set at naught;
And when your name was much defamed,
    you never vengeance sought.

While others strove for greatness,
    you stayed meekly in the shadows;
And when the wrong seemed strong,
in prayer you fought and won your battles.

Though many thrived by coarse deceit,
    you kept your motives pure;
Dishonest gain you ne'er allowed
    your vision's light to blur.

Your counsel was belittled,
    but from malice you stayed clean;
And when some said, *God's left you,*
    harder on Him you did lean.

It's like a pain that's lost its sting,
    like broken wings that fly—
A transformation which occurs
    when one to self has died.

A grain of wheat falls to the earth,
    is buried 'neath the soil;
The Sower wills that it but die,
    not that it strive or toil.

Were this small seed to have a voice,
it might cry, *This is best?!
I'm small, I know, but if I die
I'll be worth even less!*

The dampness of this place
will surely hasten my demise;
My vision's been destroyed by dirt
that's fallen in my eyes.

I love to be where others are …
why must I be alone?
I'm blanketed by darkness—
I will die as one unknown.

My self is all that I have left—
I've tried so hard to shield it;
It's every bit of who I am,
and yet I'm asked to yield it.

I want to live a fruitful life—
can't death be told to wait?
I have to die to really live?
There must be some mistake!

But then one day, the protests cease,
of contest there's no trace;
The seed, with one last feeble sigh,
succumbs to death's embrace.

Where 'twas the battle with the will
and questions of design,
'Tis now a final whisper,
Not my will be done, but Thine.

Within the darkness of its death,
a miracle unfolds;
And after many days
emerges fruit of shining gold.

Just as the tiny seed,
we may not reap earth's quick rewards,
Of riches seen, of praises heard,
of bounty's store outpoured.

But often what the world ignores
is what all heaven sees:
The lonely struggle with our will,
small gains, and bended knees.

Surrendering, we overcome;
in losing, still we win;
In fully dying to ourselves,
in Christ we live again.

*Except a corn of wheat fall into the ground and die,
it abideth alone: but if it die, it bringeth forth much fruit.*
John 12:24 KJV

Our Heavenly Father's Care

*The secret of peace is the constant referral
of all things to the care of God.*
Unknown

The road I walk sometimes seems long,
though far I cannot see;
Just light enough for one more step,
the Father grants to me.

I do not know what lies ahead,
the past I leave behind;
But all I need today,
within the Father's hand I find.

When doors are closed, and gone
seem all my opportunities,
Why pace and ponder in distress?
The Father holds the keys.

Though I am prone to plan my way
and choose each of my steps,
The Father in His loving wisdom
often redirects.

When faced with problems, oft I feel
alone and much dismayed;
And then the Father says again,
I'm here—don't be afraid.

I dare not ever lean upon
the frail arm of flesh,
But in the Father's arm of strength
I trust and safely rest.

There's much I do not know
concerning troubles which befall,
But it's enough to realize
the Father knows it all.

Though all of earth forget me,
cast me off disdainfully,
Secure within the comfort of
the Father's love I'll be.

I would not welcome pain and loss
nor choose all things that be;
Yet with the Father all I leave,
for He does care for me.

*Casting all your care upon Him,
for He cares for you.*
I Peter 5:7 NKJV

A Heartbeat of His Handiwork

I hope your life will be as beautiful
as it was in the mind of God
when He first thought of you.
Unknown

Why was I born? What purpose holds
my life upon this earth?
Will what I say and do while here
have more than little worth?

The world spins on and all its seasons
come and go the same;
Does God, Who made all things existing,
know me by my name?

He seems so great and I'm so small,
He's strong and I am weak;
He knows all things before they be,
but I must knowledge seek.

The future is more clear to Him
than is to me the present;
Perspective for Him is complete,
but mine a shadowy crescent.

The nations are before Him,
yet my world at best is small;
Would He Who rules the Universe
e'en hear me when I call?

He walks with ease on stormy seas,
I stumble at a thought;
He worries not for anything,
with cares my mind is fraught.

Almighty, naught besets Him,
but I shrink from my own fears;
Can He Who bids the rains to fall
be mindful of my tears?

His simplest ways do far exceed
my noblest fabrications;
His smallest thought brings shame
to my most wise imaginations.

So oft when He says *no*,
my reasoning heart thinks rather *yes;*
And when I'm prone to say *right now* ...
To wait, He says, *is best.*

What have I then, and who am I
that such a One as this
Should even notice what I do
or care that I exist?

For God so greatly loved the world …
the Bible long has stated;
But I am like a grain of sand
among this throng created.

Then comes to me a voice so still
my heart alone can hear—
The voice which soothes the troubled mind,
bids weary travelers cheer:

My child, I am your Maker—
I have heard your searching thoughts;
I know each sigh you've made
and every answer you have sought.

'Twas I Who saw your tears
and strove with peace your soul to flood;
I bathed your wounds in oil
and bound them with My cords of love.

I felt each disappointment,
knew each time your heart was crushed;
And in temptation's heat,
I bade a breeze your face to touch.

I knew you e'er I formed you—
yes, I even knew your name;
I gave to you the breath of life,
when from the womb you came.

I formed you with the hands which made
the heavens and the earth;
And e'er I hung the world in space,
I planned your day of birth.

The blueprint I've drawn up for you,
none else can ever fill;
'Twas fashioned with much love and care
according to My will.

I made you in My likeness,
My approval only seek;
Compare yourself with no one else—
you're wonderfully unique!

'Twas nothing wrought at random,
all your features I prescribed:
Your height, your hair, your nose, your voice,
the color of your eyes;

Abilities, mentality,
your personality,
Your family, and your time on earth,
your nationality.

Though most will tend to measure worth
by outward beauty fair,
Don't be distressed about the "shell"—
My focus isn't there.

It rests within, down in the soul,
where only I can see;
It's there I long to find a heart
that's yielded unto Me.

What brings Me greatest joy is when
I in your nature see
The beauty of My character
in unfeigned purity.

The heart reflects upon the face,
the soul within the eyes;
And actions are what show the world
what in your spirit lies.

You've wondered what your purpose is
and what's your real worth …
It's simply that I, through your life,
be glorified on earth.

All that you have I've given you—
in Me let your boast be;
Scarce is the worth of what you do
and are apart from Me.

I long to draw you closer,
so that you might really know Me;
You'll never be the same again—
My presence changes wholly.

Deep wisdom graces all My choices—
I've made no mistakes;
And patiently, My soul
the finished product now awaits.

If you will daily seek Me
and submit your will to Mine,
My plan I will reveal and guide you
one step at a time.

I only ask that you give back
the life I've given you;
And as you wholly trust Me,
you will find Me wholly true.

O Lord, You have searched me and known me.
You know my sitting down and my rising up;
You understand my thought afar off.
You ... are acquainted with all my ways.
Psalm 139:1–3 NKJV

A Journey of the Heart
Based on Psalm 23

*The beginning of a wrong situation in my life
will reveal my faithfulness to God;
the ending of a wrong situation in my life
will reveal God's faithfulness to me.*

Another disappointment—
one more dream that's washed ashore;
Another *no* from heaven,
and another closing door.

Hope seems as but a flicker,
faint the beacon of my heart;
Unclear has grown the vision,
and obscure the distant mark.

I need Your hand to guide me, Lord,
Your footprints sure to tread,
Your loving arms to hold me,
and Your eyes to see ahead.

With You beside me, I'll not lack,
on Your great strength I'll lean;
You'll lead me by still waters,
make me rest in meadows green.

In valleys, You'll restore my soul
and lead in paths of right;
And though I walk through death's dark shadow,
I'll not fear the night.

For Your name's sake, You will be true,
with sovereign rod correct;
And with Your staff You'll comfort me,
support, sustain, protect.

You'll spread for me a table
and refresh my hungry soul;
With oil You'll anoint my head,
my cup will overflow.

Your goodness and your mercy
all my days shall follow me;
And in Your glorious presence,
I shall dwell eternally.

Keep your heart with all diligence,
for out of it spring the issues of life.
Proverbs 4:23 NKJV

Saved by Hope

The Tree Story
Luke 13:6–9

The root of a thing, being visible to none,
reveals its condition through its fruit,
being visible to all.

A breeze plays gently in the trees,
soft clouds float 'cross the skies;
The orchard seems alive with joy—
the Dresser has arrived!

His garments glisten like the sun,
as He begins to wend
Between the trees—His Father's trees—
He knows each one of them.

Sometimes a smile lights His face,
and sometimes He will nod;
Sometimes, with tool in hand, He stoops
to loosen up the sod.

While passing by, He carefully
inspects each branch's fruit;
And thereby, He well knows
in what condition is the root.

Now suddenly, He stops—
His loving face clouds with concern;
He scans the boughs before Him,
then His eyes toward heaven turn.

He vividly recalls the day
His Father looking 'round,
With gaze fixed on this tree had said,
Son, let's cut this one down.

*For three years, I've been looking
for some fruit upon its branches;
And every year, it's bore but leaves—
why give it further chances?*

*For all the sun and rain bestowed,
it's only using space;
Why longer strive when We can plant
another in its place?*

The Dresser looked with longing,
in His eye there was a tear;
And then He said, *Please, Father,
let Us leave it yet this year.*

*I'll prune it, dig around it,
and build up its soil bed;
And if it still brings forth no fruit,
We'll do as You have said.*

Now breaking from His thoughts,
the Dresser eases toward the tree;
Then tenderly, He touches it,
and says, *So let it be.*

He reaches for His tools,
speaking on in soothing tones:
*Through all these years, I've cared for you
and watched as you have grown.*

*You started as a tiny seed,
then through the earth you sprouted;
That one day you would grow up
tall and strong, I never doubted.*

*But when the day came that you should
bear fruit of quality,
With care, I checked each year
and rustling leaves were all I'd see.*

*I have much hope within Me
that with just a little help,
Your branches will burst forth with fruit …*
and then the Dresser knelt.

The spade went deep into the ground
and broke up hardened soil;
The tree was still but pensive,
as it watched the Dresser toil.

Then to the soil, He applied
an unfamiliar substance;
And as He worked it in,
the tree responded with repugnance:

That substance will but harm my roots—
it's rich with bitter sting!
How can this which invokes such pain
e'er profit anything?

The Dresser answered patiently,
I only do those things
Which ultimately fruitfulness
and lasting beauty bring.

This process, which seems painful
and of hardship to endure,
Is just what will produce choice fruit
of tender sweetness pure.

The Dresser worked a little more,
then quietly arose;
And as He reached for one last tool,
the waving branches froze.

Oh please, Sir, not the pruning shears!
implored the frantic tree;
For if You cut my branches back,
devoid of worth I'll be!

Though fruit I have not borne,
that I have grown, one can't deny;
But if You take e'en that I have,
it's certain I will die!

Believe in Me, the Dresser whispered,
as some branches fell;
If you stand strong through all,
I promise, all things will be well.

His heart was stirred with pity,
as He heard the fading pleas;
'Twas nothing more to say
that disappointment's pain would ease.

The last branch softly fell,
just as the sun began to set;
And as the Dresser turned to leave,
He gently urged, Don't fret.

All this is just as needful
as the gentle rains which fall;
If you could share My vision,
you would thank Me for it all.

The Dresser looked around once more,
then vanished in the dusk;
The tree, once clothed in beauty,
now felt stripped of even trust.

It seemed as but a skeleton,
no longer tall and strong;
It felt forsaken, all alone,
as night came stealing on.

The summer came and went,
and soon came autumn's fiery glow;
Then winter softly draped the earth
in tufts of velvety snow.

One day, the warm winds blew again,
the birds began to sing;
The earth burst forth with fresh new life,
with joy embracing spring.

The weeks continued on,
and faithfully in sun or rain,
To see how grew each much-loved tree,
the Dresser daily came.

One quiet summer morn,
amongst the trees the Dresser strode;
When all at once, He stopped—
His gentle eyes with pleasure glowed.

He stood before the one
which He had labored so to save;
And as He scanned each branch,
He saw the fruit for which He'd prayed.

𝒜 smile lit His face,
and reaching out to touch the tree,
He said with utmost tenderness,
You're of great joy to Me.

*𝒴ou did not understand just why
I did the things I did,
And why My actions seemed to counter
growth and beauty's bid.*

*𝒯he pruning of your branches
seemed as loss to you, I know;
But in the process, as I wished,
your roots did deeper grow.*

*𝒮o patiently, you suffered long,
enduring pain and loss;
But never does there come reward
unless there's first a cost.*

*𝒪ne's outward strength and beauty
will not keep in drought or storm;
Nor are they that of which rare fruit
of quality is formed.*

*𝒥n winning first within
is how to beat the outward odds;
By reaching for deep water veins,
through hard and thirsty sod;*

Still hoping, though bewildered,
trusting through the winter long—
All these engender growth,
and make your inner fiber strong.

Your fruitfulness will others bless—
sustaining strength they'll find,
From that which was begotten
when you bowed your will to Mine.

But had I altered just one step
to make an easier way,
This fruit I'd not have seen—
in fact, you'd not be here today.

Sure death for you was pending,
'til I gave all I could give;
I sacrificed My sweat, My tears—
My all ... so you could live.

He that abideth in Me, and I in him, the same bringeth forth much fruit: for without Me ye can do nothing. Herein is My Father glorified, that ye bear much fruit; so shall ye be My disciples.
John 15:5, 8 KJV

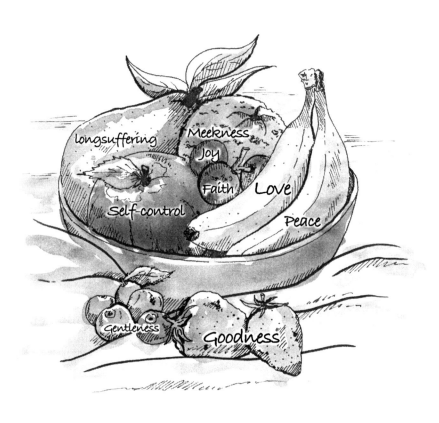

The Essence of God's Presence

*Life becomes harder for us when we live for others,
but it also becomes richer and happier.*
Albert Schweitzer

Dear Lord, I would be like You,
as I walk this earthly way;
And for the change this world needs,
let it start with me, I pray.

Help me be Your **love** to all,
though all would live for self;
Embrace through me the lonely,
wounded hearts that need Your help.

Help me be the smile of **joy**
that shines where hurt has been,
The warmth of sunbeams on the soul
that cries from deep within.

Help me be Your **peace**,
in times of trouble and distress;
Transmitting trust unshaken,
calling fearful hearts to rest.

Help me be **longsuffering**
'neath offensive stings of wrong—
To patiently endure,
'til all the wrong in me is gone.

Help me to be **gentle**,
through the pain which I have known;
To not be harsh, but kind,
as though one's feelings were my own.

Help me be Your **goodness**,
though there's evil all around;
For integrity and virtue,
Godly character renowned.

Help me be that life of **faith**,
through which You show Your power;
To know, believe, and then obey,
though mountains 'round me tower.

Help me to be **meek**,
of lowly heart and humble mind;
And as a willing servant,
may I thus true greatness find.

Help me show forth **self-control**
in feelings, words, and actions—
Submitting to Your Lordship
all my appetites and passions.

Oh, Lord, in all my living,
this my earnest prayer shall be:
Please help me die to self,
so You might wholly live through me.

*But the fruit of the Spirit is love, joy, peace,
longsuffering, gentleness, goodness, faith, meekness,
temperance: against such there is no law.*
Galatians 5:22, 23 KJV

Destined to Die?

*In loving memory
of all the precious children
who have died through needless abortions.*

It's dark inside this womb,
and only God knows that I'm here;
As yet, I'm just a tiny seed—
my gender is unclear.

But it's a start, and I can't wait
to see what I'm to be:
A boy, a girl, it matters not,
as long as I am me!

I want someday to thank the One
Whose kind hand put me here;
He must have great things planned for me—
there's nothing I need fear.

In here, I'm warm and safe—
I feel so cozy and secure;
I'll do my best to grow real fast,
of that Mom can be sure!

Time's moving right along,
and I've been here about eight weeks;
Not long ago, I felt
my little heart begin to beat.

My nervous system, spinal cord,
and brain are all in place;
I wonder what I'll do
when I outgrow this tiny space.

Now well into my third month,
I'm not quite two inches long;
Today I moved my legs
and flexed my arms—they're getting strong!

I tested all my toes, and then
I curled up all my fingers;
I even had the hiccups—
my, oh, my, there were some zingers!

I've passed the four-month mark ...
I'm going to be a little girl;
I'm so excited—I just know
my hair is going to curl!

I'll make my mom so proud of me,
my dad will hold me tight;
If he had hoped I'd be a boy,
he'll just say, *It's alright!*

Dear Mommy had an onion
on her hamburger today ...
I tried to suck my thumb
to make my heartburn go away!

And then I kicked a tad bit hard
in stretching to full size;
I don't know if you felt it, Mom,
but I apologize.

I touched my face, my nose, my mouth …
I'm going to be a cutie!
I wonder what they'll name me …
maybe Heidi, Lynn, or Judy.

In all these weeks of being here,
my heart's not missed a beat;
This gift of life is wonderful—
a miracle complete!

A scope is shining in on me—
my small hand shields my eyes …
I've really changed in recent weeks,
I know they'll be surprised.

I smile and lift my other hand
to wave to Mom and Dad;
They must be great, the best of parents
one could ever have!

I'll help Mom make her cookies,
give her warm hugs when she cries;
I'll run through grassy meadows,
chase the breeze, catch butterflies.

I'll roller skate and ride a bike
and go on walks with Dad;
I'll skip into his arms
and kiss his nose when he seems sad.

I faintly hear some voices now,
I turn my head to listen—
I sense that something's very wrong ...
in fear, my body stiffens.

I seem to hear the doctor say,
A girl it would've been;
And now, as Mommy starts to cry,
he tells her, *Let's begin.*

I *am* a girl—I wonder why
he'd say that to my mom;
But, wait ... just down below me
I perceive this curious wand.

It's moving toward me quickly,
and it's noisy to my ears;
I pull myself away,
but it keeps coming, oh, so near!

I feel it start to pull at me ...
I tremble with alarm;
Until my birth, why can't I stay here
where I'm safe and warm?

I open up my mouth to scream,
Where are you, Mommy? Help me!
It's tearing at my limbs—
my arms and legs, so long and healthy!

Won't Daddy come and rescue me?
Is he aware of this?
Oh, no ... there goes my leg!
In pain, I tightly ball my fists.

My other leg, and now an arm ...
in agony I writhe!
This must be one way that a healthy
unborn child dies.

My will to live wanes quickly,
as my other arm's ripped free;
Now mangled inhumanely,
I am vacuumed like debris.

I've loved to dream, to be alive,
like all the wanted children;
But some of us don't have that choice,
when someone says, *Just kill them!*

Since God, alone, created me
and formed me with His hand,
Why don't I have the right to live
according to His plan?

I cry with pain, my sad heart breaks,
my strength is almost gone;
I thought my parents loved me,
but I now know ... I was wrong.

Why Mommy would allow *this,* though,
I'll never understand;
I guess this must be what is called
"Abortion on Demand."

I gladly would have filled
another's empty arms that ached,
If Mommy thought my being here
was just a bad mistake.

My little body was brand new—
I had so much to give;
Why do I have the right to die ...
but not the right to live?

For You formed my inward parts; You covered me
in my mother's womb. I will praise You, for I am fearfully
and wonderfully made; marvelous are Your works ...
My frame was not hidden from You ... Your eyes saw my substance,
being yet unformed ... How precious also
are Your thoughts to me, O God!
Psalm 139:13–17 NKJV

Trampled Treasures
A Loving Tribute to the Elderly

The young strive to be beautiful,
so bold and brave of heart—
The aged dare to let experience
wisdom's grace impart.

They're rocking softly in their chairs ...
so silent ... so alone ...
Absorbed in treasured memories
of this place they've called their home.

They'd met while still in school,
all those many years ago;
Just how and when their love began,
they didn't seem to know.

Unplanned, their eyes had locked one day—
A pretty face, thought he;
And blushing softly 'neath his gaze,
A fine young man, thought she.

Thereafter was each ballgame played
with fervent heart and hand,
By he who knew a bright-eyed beauty
watched him from the stands.

She soon began to notice
he would leave his group of friends,
And ask if he might walk her home
from school now and then.

When she was by his side,
he wondered why the world stood still;
And why her smile so sweet
would make his heart race 'gainst his will.

Soon graduation came,
and both had gone their separate ways;
But neither could forget
that spark of love from school days.

One day, there came a letter,
followed by a small bouquet;
He wished to see her once again,
to which she said, *You may.*

Their friendship sweetly grew,
and then he brought a single rose …
With one hand gently holding hers,
he lovingly proposed.

There were no two on earth
who were more lost in love than they,
As they pledged to be true 'til death
upon their wedding day.

The years slipped by, through thick and thin,
through evens and through odds;
Yet stronger grew their love
and their sustaining faith in God.

Divorce was not an option—
not in word or smallest thought—
Because they'd vowed their love for life
the way the Bible taught.

Their lives were hard back then,
as they grew crops of hay and corn;
And still more scarce their funds became,
as each new child was born.

But yet, they shunned dark, selfish schemes
of cruel abortion's bid;
For just as each life was conceived,
each had the right to live.

So side by side, they raised
their seven precious girls and boys;
Together they had stayed and prayed,
through heartaches and through joys.

They served their country faithfully,
paid taxes as required;
And during wartime scarcities,
they'd sacrificed desires.

Their church and small community
and friends in need soon learned,
If possible, they'd help,
expecting nothing in return.

All things had not seemed fair and right,
as life and time progressed;
But yet, their God and fellowmen
they loved and served no less.

Their children all had married,
now had families of their own;
But jobs and opportunities
had called them far from home.

They knew their family loved them,
yet somehow, that helped but little;
And many nights, a lonely tune
was heard from Papa's fiddle.

They watched their country segregate
the youthful from the aged;
And with a chill, they first pronounced
the word, called *euthanasia*.

They'd beat the Great Depression,
weathered floods and drought and war;
Yet many folks thought that they were
not worth much anymore.

Illegal aliens, welfare vagrants,
bled the land's reserves;
And housed in comfort, crimnals cried
for luxuries they "deserved."

But they who'd worked hard, given much,
and helped to shape the nation,
Were targets of disdain, contempt,
and hostile degradation.

They're helpless burdens, bothersome,
sad liabilities …
Conveyed a culture's attitudes
that'd learned to kill with ease.

Their rocking ceases as they now
look in each other's eyes;
Each seems to know the other's thoughts—
no questions, no replies.

He rises, then he kneels beside
his lovely aging bride;
Just as before, his sad voice breaks,
our God will be our Guide.

*Though all of earth reject us,
heaven holds for us a place;*
Their tears begin to mingle,
as they pray in close embrace.

Though difficulties lie ahead,
they'll see them through together;
In all of life, they'll hold the hand
of He Who holds forever.

*The silver-haired head is a crown of glory,
if it is found in the way of righteousness.*
Proverbs 16:31 NKJV

America: From Triumph to Tragedy

*The spiritual condition of the church
always determines the moral condition of the world.*
Ron Auch

Framed against an azure sky,
unfurled in proud display,
Gracefully waves, in red, white, and blue,
the flag of the USA.

Though bought and sold across the land,
its true worth scarce is told;
For shadowed 'neath its beauty
rest the strong and brave of old.

Great husbands, fathers, brothers, sons,
and sweethearts gave their lives,
To capture for their country
freedom's noble, costly prize.

With bold, unflinching passion,
Patrick Henry made his cry:
Give me liberty—or give me death!
For freedom's cause he'd die.

Did we so soon forget
the cold, dark days at Valley Forge,
When weary, dying soldiers knelt
and prayed, *Please, help us, Lord*?

Outnumbered were their armies,
but their hearts with purpose swelled;
Their quest was one worth living for
and dying for as well.

But what has happened to the ground
they fought with blood to gain?
In God We Trust has been displaced
by humanism's reign.

The Bible, once our children's text,
our leaders' handbook, too,
Is now disdained for public use
by all but just a few.

Prayer, our onetime source of strength,
is oft reproached as well;
Bold, angry liberals burn our flag—
yes, cracked is freedom's bell.

True justice seems forgotten,
as our courts take sides with crime;
While wrong is praised and right is shunned
to stay with changing times.

Our government is rocked by fraud,
our churches reel from scandals;
Our cities are dark habitats
for murderers and vandals.

Large television shrines
make family altars hard to find;
Diseases without cures
conclude our nation's dread decline.

Life is no longer promised to
the unborn and the aged;
The Declaration, *Life ... for all ...*
has died on history's pages.

How long can liberty withstand
the inward slow decay,
Of strengths becoming weaknesses,
of anchors giving 'way?

Our nation hangs by mercy's thread,
our hope is but to pray,
And turn again to righteousness—
God help the USA.

Righteousness exalts a nation:
but sin is a reproach to any people.
Proverbs 14:34 NKJV

*I sought for the answer to the greatness of America.
I sought her greatness in her cities, her factories,
her rivers and lakes, her mountains, her waterfalls,
her seaports, and halls of government.
I did not truly understand the greatness of America
until I visited her churches and witnessed
her pulpits aflame with righteousness.
America is great because she is good—
if America ever ceases to be good,
then she will cease to be great.*

Alexis de Tocqueville–1830s
Early Nineteenth Century
French Ambassador to America

Come, Lord Jesus

The greatest work that God has ever done
is not preparing heaven for man
but preparing man for heaven.
Dale Yocumb

This earthly road seems long, dear Lord,
with trials not a few;
How long 'til heartaches cease
and we come home to be with You?

To see Your precious face
would far surpass earth's fleeting pleasures;
To be with You forever
worth much more than all earth's treasures.

Lord Jesus, please, come quickly,
let dark evil's day be past;
What blissful joy—the thought of being
home with You at last!

Surely I come quickly ...
Even so, come, Lord Jesus.
Revelations 22:20 KJV

Where Are You, Lord?

*The reality of God's presence is not dependent
on any place, but only dependent upon the determination
to set the Lord always before us.*
Oswald Chambers

To You, oh God, I lift my soul
and stretch these hands of clay;
Please, bow Your ear and patiently
list to my words, I pray.

I seem to catch a glimpse of You
in all Your wondrous works;
But yet, I often wonder, Lord,
where are You when it hurts?

Where are You when the path seems long
and mist enshrouds my way?
And why must heaven seem so still,
when I kneel down to pray?

The answers to my questions
often seem just out of reach;
But why, Lord, must it be so long
e'er to me Your voice speaks?

I don't mean to complain,
but yearn to know You as You are;
I long to understand Your ways,
walk deep into Your heart.

And then a hand encloses mine,
so warm, so kind and tender;
And as my Maker speaks to me,
my lips no sound can render:

I am the mountain's majesty,
a firelight's warm glow;
I am the mighty rivers
and the whiteness of the snow.

I am the blue of summer skies,
the whisper of a breeze;
I am the roar of ocean waves,
the blaze of autumn trees.

I am the laughter of a child,
the beauty of a rose;
I am the song of birds,
the life by which a seedling grows.

I am the twinkling stars,
the brilliance of a setting sun;
I am a shining rainbow,
I'm your rest when day is done.

I am a gentle rainfall,
silvery moonlight in the dark;
I am a flower's fragrance,
I am peace for every heart.

I am the hand that lifts the load—
when you're alone, I'm there;
I am the comfort for your fears,
I am the God Who cares.

I am the hope which anchors,
I'm the air you daily breathe;
I am the love which holds you—
I am all you truly need.

There'll always be those things
that you can't seem to understand,
And moments when you'll wonder
why I changed your well-laid plans.

The choices that I make
are ever with your good in mind;
I feel your deep concerns,
but for all things there is a time.

My thoughts are different from your thoughts,
your ways are not like Mine;
But if you'll trust Me with your life,
My best you'll surely find.

*So when you wonder where I am
and if I've heard your prayers,
Remember, I am God ...
I'm there with you ...
I'm everywhere.*

*Lo, I am with you alway,
even unto the end of the world.*
Matthew 28:20 KJV

Sweeter as the Waves Go By
The Voyage

Smooth seas do not make skillful sailors.
African Proverb

I walked along the shores of time,
beside life's restless sea;
Until one day, I heard a voice
say gently, *Follow Me.*

Before me lay the world,
which beckoned with a jeweled hand;
Enticing with its dazzling flare
and promises so grand.

But then, I looked into the eyes
of He Who spoke my name …
'Twas then I met the Savior,
and my life was wholly changed.

His face with love was radiant,
His garments shone like jasper;
My heart was stirred with weeping,
as I knelt and called Him *Master.*

With tenderness, He touched me,
then I saw His hands so scarred …
Oh, Lord, I cried, *naught that You ask
will I esteem too hard!*

He kindly smiled, then lifted me
and looked out toward the ocean;
Come, follow Me, He said again,
as toward a ship He motioned.

The waiting vessel gently bobbed,
as waves rolled toward the shore;
Without a thought of looking back,
I followed Him on board.

The day was bright and beautiful,
the sky seemed ne'er so blue;
Joy filled my heart as we embarked,
and old things slid from view.

A warm breeze swept across my face,
the sails billowed taut;
This peace I felt was that for which
my soul so long had sought.

I saw the Master at the helm—
there was no need to fear;
Before I even saw His face,
I felt His presence near.

His eyes met mine as I recalled
His words e'er we set sail:
*I'll never leave you nor forsake you ...
trust Me—I'll not fail.*

There will be times of darkness,
moments fraught with winds of trial;
E'en when you cannot see Me,
I'll be with you every mile.

When tempted to abandon,
stay aboard, whate'er betide;
I know the way, and we will safely
reach the other side.

A cold wave of uneasiness
came sweeping o'er my soul;
Just then, the Master smiled at me—
my thoughts He seemed to know.

For many days we sailed,
'neath the sun and through the storms;
Though far we'd come, the Master's face
seemed neither scathed nor worn.

He reassured me often,
daily grew my love for Him;
And stronger seemed my trust,
'midst every boisterous wave and wind.

But then one night, a gale arose
much stronger than before;
I could not see the Master's face—
in fear, I cried out, *Lord!*

The waves came crashing o'er the rail,
a cold rain stung my face;
The ship was tossed from side to side,
as doubts my heart embraced.

The wind alone did answer,
as my mind groped darkly on;
Dejection's cloud engulfed me,
as I searched in vain for dawn.

Why would the Master not reply?
Did He not hear my cry?
He's left you, sneered the Tempter;
leave the ship before you die!

*You cannot see or feel Him,
and you've long not heard Him speak;
Besides, the Master's asked too much
of one so small and weak.*

My weary gaze swept skyward,
as my cold hands gripped the rail;
Fear not—I'm here, a whisper came,
above the howling gale.

The night stretched on, and gradually,
the storm seemed to subside;
Then off beyond the misty veil,
the sun began to rise.

I sank down on my knees
and peered across the slippery deck;
Against the gathering light,
I saw the Master's silhouette.

Embued with sweet relief,
I closed my eyes in calm repose;
And then I felt the Master's arms
of refuge draw me close.

He'd been there all the time,
just as He told me He would be;
And after several moments,
He said softly, *Come with Me.*

He led me to the helm,
and then exclaimed, *We're almost there!
Before too long, you'll hear the sound
of singing fill the air!*

I stood there close beside Him,
brightly following His gaze;
Beyond the dawn, I saw
the distant shore with light ablaze.

I heard love's sweetest songs,
as we drew closer to the port;
And from the shoreline, angels thronged
our vessel to escort.

The Master took my hand,
as tears of gladness washed my face;
Such peace I felt as we approached
this great celestial place.

All questions soon would vanish,
cares and trials pass away,
And painful sorrows flee,
as night changed into endless day.

I wept as I recalled
the Savior's faithfulness to me;
I loved this Man called Jesus,
gentle Master of the sea.

Oh, thank You, Lord! I whispered,
as great brilliance 'round us shone;
*You brought me safely, as You promised,
to my heavenly home!*

*Being confident of this very thing,
that He Who has begun a good work in you
will complete it until the day of Jesus Christ.*
Philippians 1:6 NKJV

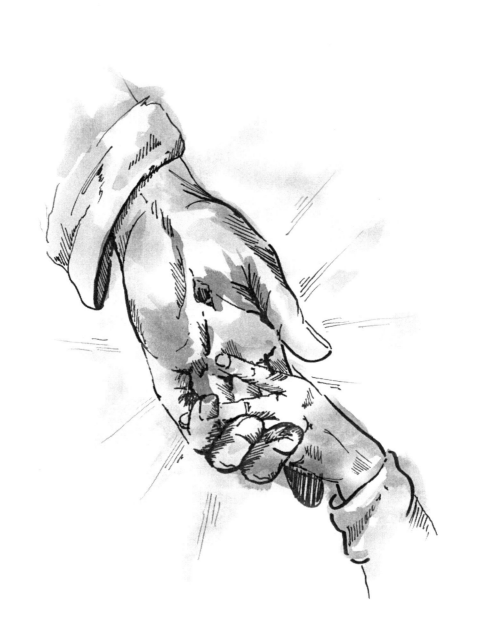

When Only God Knows

*I cannot read, I cannot pray,
I can scarcely even think—but I can trust.*
Hudson Taylor

How does one offer answers
for the tragedies we know?
How does one reassure
amidst life's questions here below?

Some things we'll never understand
this side eternity—
The steps of sorrow on our path,
the storms upon life's sea.

It seems life often does not go
the way we feel it should;
But God has promised that He'd work out
all things for our good.

These cares we must commit
into His able, loving hand,
While resting in His faithfulness,
submitting to His plan.

There is no pain but what God feels,
no tear but what He sees;
No care or disappointment had,
but what He hears our pleas.

He heals our bleeding, broken hearts,
gives beauty for our ashes;
And through these things, the image
of His Son in us He fashions.

Someday, beyond the vale of tears,
set free from every test,
What once we saw in part,
we then will understand the rest.

*And God will wipe away every tear from their eyes;
there shall be no more death, nor sorrow,
nor crying. There shall be no more pain,
for the former things have passed away.*
Revelations 21:4 NKJV

Suffering — the Path to Perfection

*Suffering is the difficult death process through which I
no longer hold to the earthly and the temporary,
but through which I cling evermore tightly
to the eternal.*

Why must the same path cresting mountains
lead to valleys low,
And wind amongst dense shadows
of the sun's retreating glow?
Past pinnacles fade quickly,
as the darkness like a foe
Cascades your wondering being—
you don't know which way to go.

You feel forgotten, all alone,
bereft of hope and cheer ...
Until your heart remembers,
God has promised—He is here.
His love upholds you through the night,
gives strength in days of drear;
And gently teaches you to trust,
until the way is clear.

Sometimes the plan of God
will also lead to deserts dry,
Where burning sands stretch endlessly
and hot wind stings your eyes.
In search of rain, you lift your gaze
up to a cloudless sky—
There is no water *anywhere*
your thirst to satisfy.

Beneath the blazing sun,
you labor onward, wondering, *why?*
Your lips are parched, your spirit's faint …
still God gives no reply.
Then suddenly, a wellspring—
God *had* heard your desperate cry;
But first, He chose your love to prove,
your depth of faith to try.

The road we're asked to walk is often
not the path we'd choose;
The means by which we're purified
not methods we would use.
The thorns which tear into our flesh,
the stones our feet to bruise,
We view as harmful hindrances—
their place to be refused.

So likewise did our Savior walk
a road with sorrow paved;
He knew no sin, had done no wrong,
yet hung as one depraved.
The whip, the thorns, the nails, the spear,
the stone to seal His grave,
Were not refused by even Christ—
His all in death He gave.

Despised, rejected, scorned, disgraced—
He bore it all alone;
Gone were the glad *Hosannas*
and the friends that He had known.
In death as life He suffered not
His will to sit enthroned;
He'd come to do His Father's will—
His life was not His own.

Are we then better than our Master,
greater than our Lord?
And dare we think that life should naught
of pain and grief afford?
Christ conquered by surrendering,
in passing through death's door;
If we would be like Him,
then for all self death waits in store.

We wish for joy without the pain,
reward without the cost;
We would be pure as gold,
while tightly clutching earthly dross.
We seek to win without a struggle,
gain without a loss;
We strive for glory without shame,
a crown without a cross.

And yet, to be like Jesus
is to suffer patiently,
Enduring all for His name's sake—
His will our heart's decree.
The Savior's call is still the same
and evermore will be:
*Deny yourself, take up your cross,
and follow after Me.*

*Though He were a Son, yet learned He obedience
by the things which He suffered; and being made perfect,
He became the author of eternal salvation
unto all them that obey Him.*
Hebrews 5:8, 9 KJV

Serving the Lord is an Honor

*Serving the Lord is an earthly honor
which bestows heavenly rewards.*

We each begin life's journey—
born to what, it's first unclear;
But for each life, God has
a well-planned reason why we're here.

We need not seek for recognition,
dream of being great;
We need not conquer kingdoms,
have a name men celebrate.

These things will cease to satisfy,
and soon will pass away;
But he who lives to please the Lord
hopes toward a brighter day.

We were not born to court the crowds,
great stores of wealth to hoard;
Life's basic truth is that we all
were born to serve the Lord.

It doesn't take the strong or wise,
the talented or great;
It only takes a willing heart
itself to consecrate.

In loving God and others
comes eternal, rich reward;
Oh, what an honor, what a joy,
to know and serve the Lord!

*And whatever you do, do it heartily,
as to the Lord and not to men, knowing that
from the Lord you will receive the reward of the
inheritance; for you serve the Lord Christ.*
Colossians 3:23, 24 NKJV

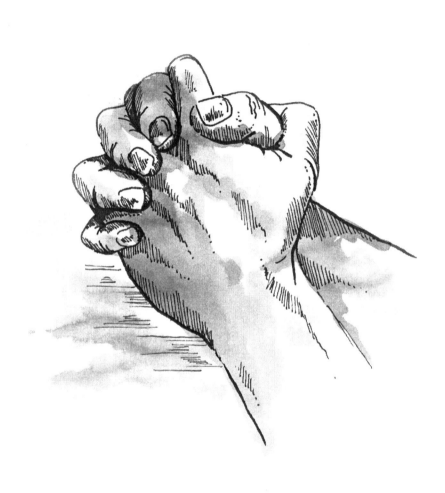

I Prayed for You

*Pray as though all of heaven and earth
were depending on you, and believe as though
all of life itself were depending on God.*

I said a prayer for you today,
when you came to my mind;
I asked the Lord to ease your cares
and help you peace to find.

I asked for you a brighter day,
a smile and not a tear;
But if a tear should come your way,
to let you feel Him near.

I asked for comfort in your pain,
His strength when you felt weak;
And in your dark'ning valley,
that your heart would hear Him speak.

And when in times of fear, I asked
His loving arms to hold you;
And if for ought you should complain,
His hands to gently mold you.

I asked the Lord to bless you
with life's necessary things,
But not so much that you should miss
the joy His presence brings.

I asked He'd redirect you,
if your feet should go astray;
To keep you in temptation,
lest from Him you slipped away.

I breathed your name in prayer
to He Who hears and answers, too—
Who said, *Cast all your cares on Me,
because I care for you.*

So give to Jesus all your cares—
your broken dreams He'll mend;
He'll light the path before you,
and He'll be your truest Friend.

He's there, He understands each need
and every trouble shares;
His touch transforms, His word renews,
His love each burden bears.

So lest you're feeling all alone,
He sent me to remind you—
That He will never leave you …
He is always there beside you.

*God is our refuge and strength,
a very present help in trouble.
Therefore we will not fear …*
Psalm 46:1, 2a NKJV

Natural Remedies for Unnatural Maladies

*Let thy food be thy medicine
and thy medicine be thy food.*
Hippocrates

We're creatures made of flesh and bone,
    just lovely works of dust;
      We're creaky and shaky,
      all wobbly and achy—
    A pill every day is a must!

God knew the weaknesses of our flesh,
    our frailties and our griefs;
      So for each need,
      He planted a seed,
To provide man and beast some relief.

He made the green herbs, the leaves and the trees,
    to be of assistance to man;
      So who ever thought
      that we could be bought
By a nice-looking carton or can?

We've long ago discarded
Granny's homemade remedies,
    For words from Doc
    and sticker shock
At our local pharmacies.

A jar of this and a box of that ...
we revel in our woes;
A hidden ache
is great,
But, oh, the drama if it shows!

We need to take a look
at some lost truths from years gone by,
When doctors worked closely
with natural things, mostly,
Extinguishing many a cry.

Oils for boils, bruises, and burns,
warm poultices, potions, and rubs;
Some sprigs of green
and tonics mean,
An herbal detox for your blood.

Bring roots and fruits for juicing,
boil some berries and bark for teas;
Create bitter brews
and hair-curling stews,
Use vinegar for arthritic knees.

To sleep well, use some honey—
add some lemon juice for coughing;
Fatigued to the core,
eat seafood galore,
Then park your new car and go walking.

There's something for babies, for toddlers, and teens,
for young adults, grandparents, too;
What's bitter makes better—
things work best together,
When lived by the tried and the true.

There's much we can do to improve our conditions
and live happy, healthier lives;
Toward wellness, be zealous,
for history will tell us
That one never wins 'til he tries.

*[God] causes the grass to grow for the cattle,
and herb for the service of man ...*
Psalm 104:14 KJV

The Heart of the Matter

We are all contributors of another's destiny,
toward success or failure,
be it good or be it ill.

We wake each morning, thinking of
the things we'll do and say;
But what if we instead would pray,
Lord, You *direct my day*?

You know the ones I'll meet today,
the lonely and afraid;
The broken hearts and lives,
the burdened souls which bow dismayed.

Please, help me take a little time
apart from life's routine,
To share a smile or lend a hand,
help someone find their dream.

If we could hear as Jesus hears
and see life through His eyes,
A breath of heaven we might bring
to countless hurting lives.

A simple act of kindness,
in a world grown harsh and cold,
Could make the difference in the next
successful story told.

Compassion toward the one who hurts,
respect toward those who lead;
Deferring selfish interests
to bestow on one in need.

Be gentle in your dealings
and sincere with all you meet;
Show loyalty in rough times,
and when wronged, be always sweet.

Waste not when you have plenty,
for it leaves more to be shared;
Be faithful with what's least,
and for much more you'll be prepared.

Be patient with the one who has not
reached perfection's peak …
Rememb'ring with humility
your own faults when you speak.

Speak only well of others,
or speak not of them at all;
Be merciful of mind toward them,
lest you be next to fall.

Encourage those who falter,
by your faith all doubt deflect;
Be cheerful 'midst great hindrances—
God's greater plan expect.

With courage, face your hardships,
for they all will pass with time;
And you'll become a voice of hope
to those who come behind.

Endure the dark and difficult,
in God's strength—not your own;
Stand tall for moral excellence—
mind not that you're alone.

Embrace a servant's heart,
with joy assist in others' tasks;
Do more than what's expected,
long before you're even asked.

Do everything wholeheartedly,
and all as unto God;
A work of love it then becomes—
not just a dreaded job.

Mistreat not those who trouble you,
for God's at work through them;
Perfecting in you His own nature,
so you'll be like Him.

Be always truthful when you speak,
and others' trust you'll earn;
Be cautious—make wise choices—
render good at every turn.

Be caring and considerate
of what another's feeling,
And keep his point of view in mind,
though yours seems more appealing.

Stay calm in times of crisis,
for your God is always there;
And never be ashamed to take
your cares to Him in prayer.

Show warmth toward those whose
hearts are cold,
and smile though others frown;
Become that right-side-up for one
whose world is upside-down.

The code of conduct's simple ...
that I always do and be
The same to others that I'd have
them do and be to me.

We need to bear each other's burdens,
weep with those who weep;
And also share the joy of those
who've overcome defeat.

God never meant for us to live
as though we were alone;
For true success is wrought
in generous deeds toward others shown.

We're helped in helping others,
and in blessing we are blessed;
In giving with an open hand,
we then receive God's best.

Let your light so shine before men, that they may see your good works and glorify your Father in heaven.
Matthew 5:16 NKJV

The Freedom of Forgiveness

*Forgiveness is a choice which I choose to make
during my circumstances. My circumstances will become
my steppingstone ... and not my tombstone.*
Pastor Kenny Carpenter

We all desire happy lives,
of pain and sadness free;
But for each one that's born,
such will not be reality.

Because of sin, each one will hurt,
and each of us will cry;
And when we wish to know the truth,
someone will tell a lie.

Life many times will seem unfair,
we'll sting from wrongs imposed;
And we'll stare hard at doors
which some unfeeling soul has closed.

We can't control what others do,
nor what they think and say;
But when those trying moments come,
we can decide to pray.

The wrongs which others do to us
need not decide our fate;
But through forgiveness, we can choose
the path our lives should take.

Forgiveness means not holding on,
but rather setting free
The one whose hurtful words and actions
have imprisoned me.

To not forgive hurts no one
quite as much as it hurts us;
We'll cease to love and laugh,
to live and give, to grow and trust.

The unforgiveness we accept
will blind our eyes from truth;
It hardens hearts and torments minds,
makes lies—not facts—its proof.

Why would we choose to hold a grudge
and dig ourselves a hole?
For hatred will but burn
an ugly crater in our souls.

To harbor bitter feelings
does not change the face of pain;
It only steals our joy
and will our true potential maim.

It doesn't change the one who wronged us
nor the thing he did;
But it will change our attitudes,
in each day that we live.

With each experience, we can choose
to focus on our loss;
Or we can rather choose to see
the gain, despite the cost.

The one will leave us bitter,
and thus hasten our demise;
The other leaves us better—
self-destruction it decries.

Forgiveness does not often happen
simply overnight;
Instead, it is a process of
repeatedly choosing right.

We'll need to hold our tongues at times
when we would rather not;
To let the past remain behind
and not our future blot.

Though showing kindness won't seem
easy,
love will always win;
And from it will emerge a place
where new ties can begin.

Though hurts will reappear at times
and bid for us to notice,
Still may our quest toward better things
and higher places hold us.

And when our memories bring them back,
let's choose to let them rest;
So that the bitterness they bring
won't keep us from life's best.

These hardships help in making us
the people we're to be,
To young and old, examples
of the highest quality.

And when we're tempted to complain
and just throw up our hands,
Remember, there is One Who suffered
more than any man.

He was the One most criticized,
the most misunderstood;
But He retained man's need at heart,
and kept on doing good.

And while He hung in agony,
His heart of love stayed true;
When praying, *Please forgive them,
for they know not what they do.*

Our Savior does not ask us
to do something He's not done;
And therefore, He knows how to aid us,
as we overcome.

If we would be forgiven
for the wrongs which we have done,
Then we must show forgiveness
to all other guilty ones.

There's ever been but One
Who did no wrong and knew no sin;
And He's the One Who'll light the way
and mend our hearts again.

The trying circumstances,
which have pow'r to bring us down,
Instead, become the substance
by which winners gain their crown.

Forgiveness leaves us clean inside
and washes hurts away;
And lets us see the beauty
of another lustrous day.

It sets us free from slavery,
shatters guilt, defeat, and pain;
And 'neath the cross of Christ,
we will prevail, in Jesus' name!

And be ye kind one to another,
tenderhearted, forgiving one another,
even as God for Christ's sake hath forgiven you.
Ephesians 4:32 KJV

A Trust to Treasure
A Note to a Friend

*A friend is the embodiment of completeness
within the entirety of another's mortal existence.*

Some people come and go,
like waves upon an ocean shore;
While others softly linger …
then they, too, are there no more.

And then there are the ones
who walk into your life one day;
So unpretentious in their ways—
you know they've come to stay.

The clouds give way to sunshine,
misty rainbows follow after;
The rain becomes as crystals,
as your sadness turns to laughter.

You needn't be someone you're not,
nor fake your smiles and tears;
Nor wonder if they'll still be there,
when days have changed to years.

Their love is strong as steel,
gentle as the morning dew;
As pure as gold and sure to hold,
so selfless and so true.

When questions fill your heart
and things seem so unfair and wrong,
Their words are reassuring
and their proffered arm is strong.

They always keep your best in mind,
they take the time to care;
And when you need someone to listen,
they are always there.

They love you as you are,
they show forgiveness, lavish praise;
They add new meaning to your life
and brighten up your days.

This kind of friend's a gift from God,
someone you won't forget;
Time spent with them is precious—
not a moment of regret.

Just as earth's hidden treasures,
lasting friends like this are few;
And that's the kind of special friend
that God gave me in you.

A friend loveth at all times ...
Proverbs 17:17 KJV

A Farewell to Friends

I can no other answer make but thanks,
and thanks, and ever thanks.
William Shakespeare

The time has come to bid farewell
to those of you I've known;
My life's been so enriched
by all the kindness that you've shown.

Your friendship and your caring ways
have come to mean so much;
Your love in times of hardship
was to me like heaven's touch.

So gratefully indebted,
I, indeed, will always be;
But may God evermore repay
this debt of love for me.

A world of thanks for all you've done—
God's very best to you;
Farewell, my friends … auf Wiedersehen …
so long … Godspeed … Adieu.

My love be with you all in Christ Jesus.   Amen.
I Corinthians 16:24 KJV

So You're Sweet Sixteen

*Dedicated to the sweet young girls around the world
who are preparing to cross the threshold into womanhood.*

Within your hands you possess
a storehouse of great wealth,
which has yet been untouched
by the ruthless fingers of hurt,
disappointment, and heartache.

Clutch it tightly,
for it was given to you
as an enrichment of your youth
and as an invaluable asset
to the years beyond.

Your virtue, mystique, and chaste femininity
are among the priceless treasures
which God has bestowed upon you
as His great gift to you;
what you do with this vast wealth
will become your gift back to Him.

Guard it with your life
and with all the strength
which you possess in God;
for once it is gone,

its contents can never be retrieved,
except they bring with them
the physical, emotional, and spiritual scars
which are an inevitable part of a wrong choice made
in a fleeting and unanticipated moment of time.

Live your life in the way
that will permit you to courageously face
the brightening sunrise of a future,
which has remained unsoiled
by a past of regrets.

Life is so short
and each moment so precious.
Live each day with care,
bathe every matter in prayer,
and trust in God with every fiber of your being;
for in Him is your hope, your fulfillment,
your love, and your life …
for today,
tomorrow,
and forever.

Remember now your Creator in the days of your youth,
before the difficult days come, and the years draw near
when you say, I have no pleasure in them.
Ecclesiastes 12:1 NKJV

None Other Like Mother

*Dedicated to all loving mothers ...
and to the memory of my sweet mom,
Mary Ellen Christner
1935–1997*

A mother's love is a gift from God
and far beyond compare
To fleeting things like wealth
and costly homes and jewels rare.

Its substance is instead comprised
of lasting things like prayer,
A listening ear, her time, a touch,
a smile which says *I care;*

A soiled apron, work-worn hands,
the smell of baking bread,
A tender hug at times
when there is nothing to be said.

It moves within the patient hands
that scour little ears,
That wash the dishes, sweep the floors,
and dry a child's tears.

Its selflessness is oft expressed
through absence of complaint;
She lends a hand when she needs one,
uplifts, though she feels faint.

The laundry piles grow,
as do the stacks of clothes to mend;
One task completed, more to go—
there seems to be no end!

She holds a lonely vigil
by a fretful sleeping child;
She answers endless questions,
sings away wee little trials.

A mother's love performs those duties
others think too tough;
She gladly does without so that
her family has enough.

She's oft the first to rise at dawn,
the last to sleep at night;
She's one who's firm but gentle,
daily teaching wrong from right.

A mother's love does not resent
long hours on her knees—
The vital force behind the scenes
by which her home succeeds.

She's willing to lay down her life
and pay whate'er the price,
To raise up Godly children
who would live and die for Christ.

As years go by, she learns
some special skills to moms akin,
Like sleeping with an open eye
'til everyone is in.

She often knows what isn't seen
and hears what's not been said;
It seems her intuition's
always just a step ahead.

It is her joy to be there,
when a voice calls out, *I'm home!*
She's one who knows, but cares not,
that her life is not her own.

For just awhile, a mother holds
her babies in her arms;
But all through life, she'll hold them
in her heart with love so warm.

These children are her charge from God,
her very flesh and blood;
The offspring of her husband,
whom she walks beside and loves.

She is a faithful friend by day,
a guiding light by night;
In rain, she's love's umbrella,
and in sunshine, joy's delight.

Her job sometimes seems thankless,
without trophies or awards;
But one day will her children call her
Blessed of the Lord.

Her husband, too, will praise her,
for there'll never be another
So qualified, so capable,
to be a mom ... like Mother.

Who can find a virtuous woman?
for her price is far above rubies.
Her children arise up, and call her blessed;
her husband also, and he praiseth her.
Proverbs 31:10, 28 KJV

The most important occupation on earth for a woman
is to be a real mother to her children.
It does not have much glory to it;
there is a lot of grit and grime.
But there is no greater place of ministry,
position, or power, than that of a Mother.
Phil Whisenhunt

The Gift of a Dad

Dedicated to all devoted fathers ...
and to the memory of my dear dad,
Mervin Roy Christner
1936–2007

What makes a father special
in a world of changing times,
When men have lost their vision
in a role once well-defined?

Good men of honor seem so scarce,
integrity seems lost ...
With many seeking names of fame
and wealth at any cost.

We seem to have forgotten
what a real man should be,
And what an impact he will have
upon his family.

For every word a father says
and every move he makes
Will map the course and set the pace
his sons and daughters take.

A good example's vital
of the one who's caught the vision—
Who has his eye upon the goal,
whose heart burns with a mission.

He must be steadfast for the right,
though all around be wrong;
And when the world is shaking,
he must stand up tall and strong.

A father daily shows his children
how to love their mother;
And thus equips them for the task
of loving one another.

He teaches them the art of kindness,
giving when it hurts;
He shows them how to pray,
and takes them faithfully to church.

A watchful father sees the dangers
lurking in the shadows;
And like a warrior on his knees,
he'll wage and win his battles.

The sun may set and rise again,
while he is bowed in prayer;
But still he presses on—
he must not fail his children there.

By day, he teaches them God's Word,
and yet again, by night;
They are his trust from God,
and his reward when they choose right.

A dad is there to throw the ball,
to help replace a wheel,
To hunt and fish, to bike and swim,
to buy a Happy Meal.

A dad's his children's hero,
standing taller than the rest;
He's stronger, better looking—
he's the finest and the best!

He's not too proud to bend down low
in dealing with his children;
He shows them understanding,
and seeks always to upbuild them.

A dad is strong but gentle,
tough but fair at every turn;
There's much that he must teach his children—
so much they must learn!

He's got one chance, a space in time,
in shaping their young lives;
In showing them what's right from wrong,
what's foolish and what's wise.

A dad wears many hats,
and learns the skills of many trades;
He'll try to fix most anything,
for the smiles and hugs he's paid.

A dad is one who wishes
he'd earn more than what he does;
He dreams of greater things,
of doing more for those he loves.

Sometimes the road is long,
the load is great—he'd like to sigh;
Instead, he squares his shoulders,
smiles, and holds his head up high.

A dad laughs loudly when he's frightened,
bellows when he's hurt;
And when he's down with sickness,
the whole family's on alert.

He growls when he feels threatened,
softly grunts when he's content;
He mumbles when embarrassed,
jumbles words he thought you meant.

He's very territorial,
pacing with a lion's shuffle;
And just to reassure himself,
he'll flex another muscle.

He leads, he guides, he motivates,
he reaches for the stars;
And shows you how to build again,
when nothing's left but shards.

A dad may seem more clumsy
cleaning floors and threading needles,
In kissing skinned-up knees,
and saying how he truly feels.

But he's the first one called
to kill a spider, catch a mouse,
To unstop every toilet,
stalk night sounds, and fix the house.

In rain or shine, a dad is there,
the loudest in the bleachers;
All heart in every action,
best-intentioned of all teachers.

A dad is not supposed to cry—
or such is what we're told;
But for each ounce of love he has,
his heart a tear will hold.

The moment he becomes a dad,
until his dying day,
A dad he'll always be—
no one can take that gift away.

Profoundly different life becomes,
when one is crowned as *Dad;*
The love you feel burns like a fire
you never knew you had.

So rise each day and hug your children,
thank God for their lives;
Someday they'll thank you, Dad,
because they mattered in your eyes.

The world will be a better place
because you took the time,
To leave your loving imprint
on your child's heart and mind.

*And you, fathers, do not provoke your children
to wrath, but bring them up in the training
and admonition of the Lord.*
Ephesians 6:4 NKJV

*It is not great talents or great learning or great preachers
that God needs, but men great in holiness, great in faith,
great in love, great in fidelity, great for God—
men always preaching by holy sermons in the pulpit,
by holy lives out of it.
These can mold a generation for God.*
E. M. Bounds

I Miss You

*With love to my late parents,
Mervin and Mary Ellen Christner*

I thought of you today,
as I looked toward the skies so fair;
I never knew a day without you—
you were always there.
I thought of how you hugged me,
how your words would lift my cares;
And how you daily spoke my name
before the Lord in prayer.

You taught me by example,
how to trust God through the pain;
You taught me how to look for rainbows
through the clouds and rain.
You showed me how to give
when there would be no earthly gain;
When wronged, to show forgiveness,
and break hatred's cruel chain.

You said to stand, though all alone—
from duty not to shirk;
Defend the holy, right, and true,
and not God's name besmirch.
You showed me how to rally
and to rise above life's hurts;
To go the extra mile,
and to know love always works.

We learned to pull together,
when our world was pulled apart;
And how to start again,
when loss had left its heavy mark.
We learned that morning always comes,
though night seems long and dark;
And how you get through anything,
when God lives in your heart.

We often did with less,
but didn't seem to really mind …
Because our home was filled with laughter,
deeds were always kind.
The most important things
did not of gold or silver shine;
They came from deep within,
where one eternal treasure finds.

You taught me that you don't blame God
for all life's woes and ills;
Nor use inane excuses
to refuse the path He wills.
To walk with Him is not to say
the road won't be uphill;
But rather, when life twists and turns,
He'll be there with you still.

You loved me when I made poor choices,
helped me find my way;
Your strong arms held me close,
when there was nothing left to say.
Your counsel was in wisdom,
always seasoned with much grace;
And in my heart of hearts,
no one would ever fill your place.

And then one day, you slipped away …
your time on earth was done;
But first you passed the torch,
so that I, too, this race could run.
You taught me all that mattered,
e'er you faced your setting sun;
But earth no more could hold you,
when the Father bade you come.

I thought I'd never smile again,
that tears would fall forever;
I held your memory close,
and cherished times we'd spent together.
The searing pain, the grief is great,
when earthly ties are severed;
But yet, to wish you back, I couldn't—
heaven's so much better.

And still I miss you, oh, so much—
such love you had to give;
But now I must live on
the life you showed me how to live.
I'll see you in a while,
when I cross earth's final bridge …
With heartfelt thanks forever,
for the good you said and did.

*How will **you** be remembered?*

*For My thoughts are not your thoughts,
neither are your ways My ways, saith the Lord.
For as the heavens are higher than the earth, so are My ways
higher than your ways, and My thoughts than your thoughts.*
Isaiah 55:8, 9 KJV

A Mission of Love

The Story of How We Met

This poem is lovingly dedicated to …

*the treasured memory of my dear mother,
Mary Ellen Christner,
whose final gift of love breathed new life
into my waiting dreams;*

*my wonderful sweetheart,
Steve,
whose unwavering love has given me the privilege
of living out the desires of my heart;*

*the Sustenance of my life,
Jesus Christ,
Whose strong arms faithfully held me,
enabling me to hope, trust, and wait …
until it was time.*

INTRODUCTION

The setting for the following events is Sunday, October 19, 1997, in southwest Michigan, Kalamazoo and St. Joseph counties, in the towns of Kalamazoo and Sturgis. The medical facility is Borgess Medical Center, also located in Kalamazoo, and the significant room is number three fifty-four.

When thirty-year-old nursing student, Steve Harris, arrived at Borgess Medical Center on a mid-October day in 1997, he anticipated an ordinary day of helping sick patients get well. He had no idea that he was soon to cross the threshold of an encounter which would unforgettably change his life.

At the same moment, Mary Ellen Christner lay critically ill in a bed on the third floor. She, from behind the privacy curtain in her room, had heard an unidentified young man sharing his love for Jesus with her roommate. Inspired by the dynamic of his testimony and realizing that he must have been a care-provider, she began praying that God would grant her the opportunity of meeting him. A day later, He did.

When Steve met Mary in Room 354, his eyes immediately fell on the Bible at her bedside. He sensed something different about this patient and began to visit with her. Before long, a warm, caring bond had developed between them, a mother-son kind of connection. Thereafter, Steve came to visit her faithfully—even when he wasn't on rotation—reading the Bible to her, praying with her, and learning much about the things which were most important to her: her relationship with Jesus and the family whom she loved so much.

Several days went by, and finally it was Sunday. School had been difficult, and an exam was pending, so Steve thought it best to postpone his next visit with Mary until the following Monday. However, an all-knowing God had *other* plans ... and that is where this story begins.

The account of the particular Sunday in reference is accurate, with the exception of those occurrences which developed behind the scenes. There may likewise be a fair amount of correctness in the description of those facts as well, but which of us really knows? God moves in mysterious ways, using whomever and whatever He chooses in fulfillment of His divine will. Skeptics may come and go, but God will always leave behind those, such as myself, who remain as grateful eyewitnesses of His amazing faithfulness.

On November 30, 1997, having fulfilled her role in the special plan which God ordained from the beginning of time, Mary—my mother—slipped from this earth, leaving in our hearts the story which I share with you today. Although I do not even pretend to fully understand everything exactly as it transpired, nor why, I do know that, in all things, God makes no mistakes. His ways, His thoughts, and His love are infinitely the highest and the best.

Shirlisa Christner Harris

OUR STORY

To Steve—
written for our wedding day
and read at our reception,
June 19, 1999

An angel up in Heaven
stood before a towering wall;
His steady eyes scanned upwards,
then he slowly let them fall.

Another angel soon arrived,
a few words were exchanged;
And then as though assigned a task,
they looked o'er *rows* of names.

Ah, here it is! exclaimed the first;
I've found our day's assignment!
But heaven help us both
to bring all this into alignment!

They both grew still as each began
to plot a course of action;
It had to work—it mustn't fail—
not even by a fraction!

*One angel turned and said,
The task is clear, I do believe;
The girl's name is Shirlisa,
and the young man's name is Steve.*

*Each one of them have waited
and have prayed God's will to find;
God's faithful ear has heard them,
and today it is their time.*

*Shirlisa's mother, Mary,
will fulfill a major role:
She'll usher in the blending
of these two in heart and soul.*

*It seems that Mary is quite ill ...
she's 'neath a doctor's care,
Within a health facility—
Steve lately met her there.*

*He went to work one day last week,
for clinical rotation;
I had the third-floor nurse give him
room fifty-four location.*

*'Twas in that room where Mary lay
encumbered by her sickness,
And first heard Steve as he of Jesus'
loving grace gave witness.*

He's been to see her everyday,
to pray and read the Bible;
The bond they share is close
and to the plan of God most vital.

Steve knows of Mary's fam'ly,
knows her youngest daughter's single;
He'd like to meet her, but the thought
makes hope with dread to mingle.

He's prayed for just a glimpse of her—
he's "not all spirit," he said;
He'd like to see just what exists,
before he moves ahead.

Now Mary seems to realize
what God's about to do;
She's prayed so long for one like Steve,
who's Godly, kind, and true.

He's very selfless, caring,
always quick to lend a hand …
And today, upon that basis,
will a woman meet her man.

We need to note a difference here
within their human traits:
Shirlisa's seldom early,
but now Steve is seldom late.

Today we'll see that clearly,
when we go to make this work;
We'll have to firmly interrupt
Steve's cherished drive to church.

We'll have him go to Borgess
to encourage Mrs. Christner;
Shirlisa, too, will be there
with her father and her sister.

He'll try to hold us off
because he'll want to be on time;
I may just have to knock him out
and make the driving mine.

I think, however, that he will
from time concerns defray,
When he considers how he might
make someone else's day.

The second angel finally said,
Let's go and make our start;
This mission isn't for the slow,
the weak, or faint of heart.

We've got a lot of work to do …
we'll need to pull some strings;
When this is all completed,
we'll have surely earned our wings!

So with a silent, graceful ease,
the plan was brought from heaven,
On the nineteenth of October,
nineteen hundred and ninety-seven.

The chill of fall hung in the air,
the trees with color glowed,
As these two beings stole
to St. Joe County's Borgert Road.

Shirlisa, with her father,
sister, brother-in-law, and John,
Appeared to soon be leaving
to go spend the day with Mom.

The angels then invisibly
escorted them through traffic;
John's driving skills seemed flawless,
so adept and undramatic.

The carload glided safely
to their northward destination;
The work had just begun,
for this angelic delegation.

The group soon disappeared behind
the center's tall glass doors,
Then up three floors and down the hall
to room three fifty-four.

When all seemed well, the silent beings
turned and went their way;
For on this Sunday morning,
there was no time for delay.

They moved on to Christ Temple,
where Steve sat within the service;
Their presence close beside him
didn't seem to make him nervous.

They left with him when he went home ...
they watched him *everywhere;*
While eating dinner, studying—
he knew not they were there.

At five o'clock, an angel whispered,
Let's be leaving, Steve;
Steve eyed the clock, then jumped up, saying,
Oooh, I need to leave!

*If I should climb McKinley,
walk the Gobi, crawl to Paris,
Forbid the day someone should say,
"There goes the late Steve Harris!"*

So out he ran to start his car,
and down the road he cruised—
While dodging slowpokes, moaning red lights,
with no time to lose!

It wasn't long before an angel
whispered in Steve's ear,
Now go see Mary—pray with her!
the unctioning was clear.

I can't be late for church,
thought Steve while waiting at a light;
*I have to show up early—
I'm an usher there tonight!*

The car soon left the light behind ...
the angel spoke again:
*Just go see Mary up at Borgess—
treat her as a friend.*

Steve contemplated, then again
thought,
*No, I don't have time!
I'll stop tomorrow after class—
right now, I'm in a bind!*

The angels soon exchanged
a very stern and worried gaze;
They'd have to take control,
and knock this Steve into a daze.

Just one more time they'd try,
while moving into their positions ...
They would not take *no* for an answer,
under these conditions!

Steve, go see Mary in her room!
the angel urged once more;
*Encourage her and pray with her—
that's what God's called you for!*

As Steve began objecting,
since time was not on his side,
The angel's last-ditch effort
was to interrupt and chide:

*Until this time, you've never put
yourself before another;
So don't start now when there's a need
with this dear wife and mother!*

Steve *instantly* responded,
turning sharply at the wheel,
And cut a car off in his haste—
that voice had seemed so real!

The angels chuckled heartily,
as Steve snapped into action;
He'd saved them all some trouble,
thought the two with satisfaction.

The sight of Borgess soon announced
the end to his fast trip;
Five twenty-five, his watch displayed—
he'd have to make it quick!

He parked his car and ran inside
and caught an elevator;
His nerves felt like they were aboard
an endless escalator!

Eventually, the doors slid open …
Steve was on third floor;
He hurried off and raced on down
to room three fifty-four.

The angels watched with interest,
as he turned into the room …
Then skidded to a stop as though
he'd seen men from the moon!

The room was *full* of visitors—
there was *no way* he'd stay!
The muscles in his body flexed
to carry him away.

An angel nudged Shirlisa,
who looked up with cordial calm;
And to the stranger said, *Come in—
you're here to see our mom?*

In visible discomfort,
Steve approached with halting stride;
The angels leaned against a wall—
their moment had arrived.

Soon Mary turned to look,
and smiling warmly said, *Oh, hi!*
She seemed to know him well—
this was no ordinary guy.

The two of them spoke briefly,
e'er began the introductions;
The angels watched things closely
to prevent *all* interruptions.

Then Mary called each one by name,
who stood within the room;
And one by one, Steve shook their hands …
Shirlisa's turn came soon.

When Mary spoke her daughter's name,
Steve's mind went out for tea;
He never met her gaze until
she smiled, and said, *That's me.*

He scanned her face for one brief second,
smiled, and shook her hand;
Then moved on quickly, as he prayed,
Lord, help these legs to stand!

Shirlisa, now, had noticed
this man's quiet inner strength;
For while he spoke with others,
she had studied him at length.

A fine young man, indeed he is ...
his standard's high, I'm sure;
He doesn't seem to need a wife,
she thought with some demure.

He doesn't even notice me ...
and when he takes his leave,
I'm sure we'll never meet again,
myself and this man, Steve.

And when Steve bade good-bye to all,
he looked right past the girl;
His eyes refused to focus,
and his mind was in a whirl!

His feet no longer touched the floor,
inside he felt so *strange;*
He tried to act indifferent,
but his heart somehow had changed.

He'd never felt like this before—
he might just need to stay
Here in a third-floor bed, himself,
'til all this went away!

He now recalled some cautions
Mary gave before to him,
When she had sensed his interests
and could see his bid was in:

Become her friend, she'd said to him;
*just take things nice and slow.
Hold off on talk of marriage—
win her heart by staying low.*

So out the door Steve bounded,
e'er he messed things up but good;
And filled his post at church,
the way a faithful usher should.

His mind, however, wandered badly
through the evening service,
Back up to Borgess where he'd left
the girl he'd met from Sturgis.

Shirlisa, on the other hand,
was trying to dismiss
The thoughts of one who seemed to think
that she did not exist.

Life would continue as before …
her heart would go on beating;
Without a doubt, she'd soon forget
this unplanned Sunday meeting.

Fall darkness soon descended,
as the day came to an end;
The angels saw all safely home,
then left the earth again.

Their mission was completed,
they would take a needed break;
They knew these kids would see it through—
they had what it would take.

The next day, Mary was sent home,
but e'er she left that day,
Steve asked once more if he might send
some mail Shirlisa's way.

She willingly consented—
she had faith in what she saw;
She'd found in him a Christian friend …
and future son-in-law.

And that is how it all began
in room three fifty-four,
With letters quickly following
and phone calls by the score.

Then came the cards and thoughtful gifts,
the smiles and tears to share,
Long drives to church, romantic dinners,
and quiet times of prayer;

Bike riding and canoeing,
playing tennis, feeding ducks,
Enjoying ice cream, window shopping,
watching Hondas* rust;
(*strictly a reflection of personal preference at that time)

Eluding waves on sandy shores,
and moonlit strolls by night,
Serene rides through the countryside,
warm talks by firelight.

Like threads, these things in friendship
knit their hearts and souls together;
And then God added to their lives
a love to last forever.

That's why we're here today,
and we're so glad that you are, too;
This is our celebration
of a dream that's now come true.

We'll walk this life with faith inside,
with Jesus as our Guide—
Joined hand in hand together,
heart to heart, and side by side.

Delight thyself also in the Lord; and He shall give thee the desires of thine heart. Commit thy way unto the Lord; trust also in Him; and He shall bring it to pass.
Psalm 37:3, 4 KJV

A Tiny Glimpse of Heaven
A Letter of Love to Sweet Shelby Jo
Born July 9, 2008

Were perfection to be the yardstick
by which each of us were judged worthy of life,
none of us would be here today.

I gaze into your trusting eyes,
I study your sweet face;
I press my lips against your cheek,
and feel your soft embrace.

Your head rests on my shoulder,
I can hear each breath you take;
I kiss your little nose,
so cute and perfect in its shape.

The summer sun makes white your hair—
your wisps, a feathery halo;
Your tiny fingers touch my face,
your smile is warm and playful.

I hold you close against me,
rock you gently in my arms;
And lift a plea to Jesus,
that He'll keep you from all harm.

Your sleeping form reflects such peace,
I soon become addicted
To standing by your crib until
my weariness is lifted.

Your innocence and trust are pure,
and answer to my wonder,
Of how you sleep through summer storms,
with all their crashing thunder.

I cry as I recall
those early days before we knew
The joy God had in store for us,
when first He thought of you.

Such happiness we felt,
when we first learned of your existence;
But soon our minds went numb with fear,
as we learned of a "difference."

We cried and prayed as tests were run—
there must be some mistake!
A child with Down's syndrome?
We were sure our hearts would break.

We grieved for who you wouldn't be
and what you wouldn't do;
Our lives would be so different,
if all this were really true.

We shrank with dread when thinking
of the hard things you would bear ...
The ridicule and laughter,
cold rejection, open stares.

Accomplishments would take more time,
we'd all need lots of patience;
Achievements known as "normal"
would now be great celebrations.

Our dreams would need to be rebuilt,
our hopes for you reworked;
We'd have to give our pain to God
and move on past the hurt.

Amazed, we wondered if such was,
indeed, God's perfect plan;
So blinded by anxiety,
we could not see His hand.

The worst of what might be was told us,
as we forged ahead;
*Nine lives of ten, thus diagnosed,
will end,* the midwife said.

And though our minds were shaken,
on one thing we would not bend:
We would accept what God should give—
your life we would not end.

Abortion's not an option,
we spoke firmly to the staff;
*We'll love this child and carry her
to full-term—not just half!*

We saw you on the ultrasounds,
and heard your beating heart;
You squirmed and kicked like all the rest …
so vibrant was your start!

And as your day drew nearer,
we still had so many questions;
But to God's will we pledged our souls,
without a word's objection.

And then our wait was over,
as you came into our lives;
They placed you in my arms,
and then I looked into your eyes.

Emotion's wave engulfed me,
as I held your body close …
There's nothing can compare
to love's strong river when it flows.

My heart was yours forever,
little mattered anymore;
You had my full attention
and my vast affection's store.

That was a special moment—
one your mommy won't forget—
When all the fear, anxiety,
and sadness simply left.

You were—and are—the gift God gave,
you've been the greatest joy;
I wouldn't ever trade you
for another girl or boy.

Your daddy and your siblings
also think the world of you;
You've taught us all so much
about what's beautiful and true.

You've shown such patience in distress,
contentment with but little;
And when you're inconvenienced,
you still muster up a giggle.

Your happiness exceeds the joy
which most will ever know;
And without reservation,
you have so much love to show.

How was our family chosen
to be privileged in this way?
Our lives have never been the same,
since you arrived that day.

Your smile is worth much more than gold,
your sweetness than all fame;
Your calm and quiet spirit's like
a warm and gentle rain.

Though you may never walk
a beauty pageant's dazzling runway,
Spin like a skater's dream on ice
or win a medal someday;

You may not enter Harvard,
or address some great convention;
You may not grace a Broadway stage,
or patent some invention …

It's not those things which count
because, in time, they'll fade away;
It's what you do for Jesus,
how you brighten someone's day.

Though I'd never wish Down's syndrome
on a precious boy or girl,
I'd wish your heart of love
on every person in the world.

Through you, I've glimpsed a side of heaven
I'd not seen before;
And as you bring God's presence near,
how could I ask for more?

You're perfect in your own sweet way,
bright sunshine in our skies;
A special little blessing,
precious angel in disguise.

My heart's been changed forever—
I will always love you so,
And thank the Lord in heaven
for your life, sweet Shelby Jo.

*Jesus said, Let the little children come to Me,
and do not forbid them; for of such
is the kingdom of heaven.*
Matthew 19:14 NKJV

Shelby's 1st birthday party

Shelby, at 2, with sister, Shireena, and brothers, Stevie and Scottie.

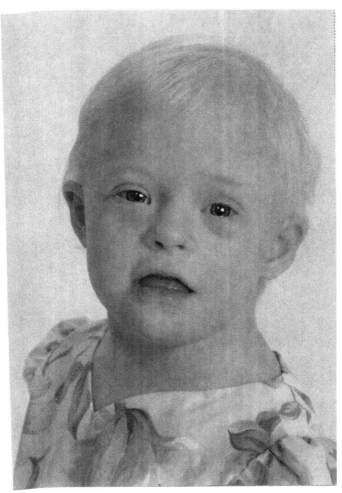

Sweet Shelby, at 28 months

CPSIA information can be obtained at www.ICGtesting.com
229624LV00001B/47/P